JOURNEY TO THE CORE

*Facing Your Worst;
Finding Your Best*

By

G. Scott Ranck

Dedication

To the people who have dared to take this journey with me:

The bride of my youth: Gayle Ranck

My mentor: Willie Pegram

My Children:

Jennifer Lyn Ranck

Lisa Ranck Dennis

Timothy Scott Ranck

Journey Mates:

Robey Landram

John Kilgore

Danny Agosto

Eric Herrin

Bay Life Men

ACKNOWLEDGMENTS

When I published my first book in 2007, I thought I was done, and that would be my life's work. I wrote a book. I was a published author. I could cross that off the *'bucket list'* and move on. But I had no idea my journey would go so deep and take so long. I was far from done! There was still much for me to learn.

Many people have encouraged me, spoke truth into my life and prodded me to write a sequel chronicling my discoveries. Knowing what I now know, there may still be more books in my future. The learning and growing should never stop.

First, I want to thank my wife, Gayle. Her never-ending support and encouragement have made me a better man. Her love and friendship are crucial in my life.

I want to thank Willie Pegram, my first mentor in the realm of emotional health. He is a good friend. Through years and miles, Willie is still only one telephone call away, day or night.

Next, I salute the Bay Life Men who are traveling this road with me. Though I don't know them all on the same level, their eagerness to listen and learn, as well as give freely of their own experiences, amazes me. One of the joys of my journey is seeing their lives transform right before my eyes. To see a man come into our group broken and sometimes weeping from life's struggles; and emerge to live a confident, humble life from their core, is so unique – an amazing gift.

And of course, thanks to my trusted friends & life associates – the readers who have volunteered to proofread my manuscript before I put it out there for the world to see. Heartfelt thanks for all their helpful suggestions and editing tips. No man is on this journey alone, and I am no exception.

Finally, thanks to the Lord Jesus, my savior, my friend, and my mentor. He is the ultimate teacher, and this is the ultimate journey!

Contents

INTRODUCTION

Many years ago, my wife Gayle and I bought a home that needed a total makeover. It was a fixer-upper, but being a builder at one point in my life, I could envision what the space could become. We tore into our new 'project,' completely gutting it: tearing out walls, cabinets, plumbing . . . Everything right down to the floor coverings.

There was only one bathroom, and it was compact. There was no space inside to expand the bathroom. So, even though the exterior of the house was brick, I decided to strip the bathroom all the way down to the 2 x 4 studs and knock out the exterior wall. I had to beat the bricks with a sledgehammer to remove them.

The house had a three-foot overhang on the roof, so I figured I could extend the bathroom at least three feet without having to do any significant roof work. Once I knocked the wall out, you could stand in the bathroom and look out to the backyard through an opening that was floor to ceiling, wall to wall- the same size as the bathroom!

We bought a one-piece fiberglass tub and shower unit that fit right in that opening. I then completed the framing and put on the exterior sheathing. We finished the remainder of the 'extreme make-over,' including a brand-new kitchen built from scratch. It was like we had a brand-new home. All the choices of colors and fabrics were our choices. The almost finished product was beautiful and inviting.

The only thing left undone was to lay the bricks on the outside of that new bathroom. Gayle would say, "Don't you think you should finish the outside?" I'd say, "It isn't a big deal. . . I'll get to it one of these days. For now, that exterior sheathing will be fine!" But I never did get around to it! We lived in that house for the next six years. That unfinished bathroom wall stuck out like a sore thumb, and it glared at me every time I was in the backyard.

After six and a half years of serving this community, an opportunity became available to our family to move to an inviting ministry in another city. We had the difficult task of selling a home in a terrible real estate market. The realtor we consulted about selling our home said, "You can't sell that house without the bricks replaced on that back wall! No bank will lend anyone the money with it in this condition."

I had no choice now. I was forced into action, but I had a real dilemma. I just wasn't sure what to do. What appeared to be procrastination on my part was not. It was honestly the fear that I didn't know how to do the brickwork. But because it had to be done, I needed to swallow my pride. I asked a trusted friend if he knew how to lay bricks. He did thank the Lord. He got me started, and I finished the job, and it looked great. I felt like a significant weight had lifted from me. It felt so good to have the entire 'makeover' finished. We got to enjoy that completed look for a couple of months before the house sold and we moved.

Gayle is so creative. From the leftover mortar, she crafted me an apple. She painted it red, put a felt base on it, and we called it my 'procrastination apple.' I put it on my desk, and it served as a reminder to me not to put things off again.

What she didn't know until years later was why I procrastinated. She didn't understand I was filled with fear and a feeling of inadequacy. I couldn't do it. I was frozen by the fear of failure. It paralyzed me to think that I just didn't have what it took to do the job. In my mind, I imagined a brick wall that would ultimately crack apart and fall. I would be exposed as an imposter! I could not move to finish the job until I had no other alternative.

My brick wall in many ways is symbolic of what multitudes of men face in their own lives every day. Many men wrestle with feelings of inadequacy, a fear of not being good enough. These feelings and concerns are the causes of why we often appear to be lazy, detached, uninvolved and disengaged; or the opposite, hyper-critical of everyone else out in front doing things, while we remain passive.

Most men are not willing to face these feelings & fears until *something* or *some event* along their journey turns their world upside down, and they have no other choice. This book is a result of my '*something*' *my* journey, a journey to my core that has taken me over a decade to unravel.

I've read widely and benefit from many good works, but ultimately this journey was the Lord and me. He used whatever He needed to reach me, reading, people and some personal encounters. The Lord and I teamed up, and both have been relentless in this pursuit.

Discovery after discovery has been made, but I always had the sense there was more to uncover. So, I kept battling, praying, asking, inviting, "*Show me Lord, and uncover the wounds and dark places.*" What kept pushing me was my apparent lack of love, joy, and peace. I am already planning my next book showing the inner workings of what it looks like when God speaks to me. Stay tuned!

When I sensed that my journey had revealed so many hard to discover issues, I had a very strong prompting that it should never take another person as long as it has taken me. "*Give them a roadmap and a tour guide, and you will reduce the time it takes a struggling man or woman to prepare for life in this world.*"

My first book, "*Connecting the Dots facing pain; finding peace,*" was written about five years into my journey. It was all I had learned up until that time. Its content is valuable as a primer for where this book, "*Journey to the Core,*" will take you.

I've learned much from others along the way. In many ways, I believe my journey has initiated me into manhood.

So, I invite you to join me on the journey to your core. I believe something extraordinary is about to happen for you. I believe as you face your worst you will ultimately find your best! The truth found here will equip you to live your life from a healthier place, from your core. That is our objective. You and I must journey to our deepest place before we can live and love from a healthy and fulfilled place. It is my prayer and hope that this book will expedite your journey!

Blessings,

Scott Ranck, December 2017

PART ONE
JOURNEY TO THE CORE

CHAPTER ONE
WHAT IS THE CORE?

The core, in this writing, is described as the bundle of all of life's positives and negatives buried deep within us. The core wounding is everything caused by living on a fallen planet. It is the enemy's efforts to block everything God intended for us to be. After working through all that damage, what is revealed at the core is who God created you to be from the beginning. The Bible calls this negative stuff sin. Sin, in this case, is a noun. It is a principle that touches every part of life. Because of this sin principle, we commit the acts of sin, which is the verb use of the word. The two concepts are different but related. Our core is a fusion of everything God intended for us to become combined with all the ramifications of the sin principle and the acts of sin committed by us and to us. Watch how these forces play out in the following story.

The young pastor sat in his study early in the morning, the sting of the elder's comments still rattling around between his ears. It seemed the people who were the leaders when the new pastor arrived had one mission in mind: stop all progress and stay in control!

The story the pastor tells himself in his head is so loud it is deafening. *"Why don't these guys spend some time and money and go to some church leadership conferences as I do? If these men ever read a book, it would be their first one. Why did they call me here to lead and then resist me at every turn? I'm so sick of facing resistance at every turn; I think I will start circulating my resume' again. Better yet, I think I may get a real job in the real world and get out of ministry altogether. Why do I always seem to run into these people everywhere I go who want to challenge everything I want to accomplish?"*

A thought pops into his mind. He remembers something he saw watching last night's news.

It was about a celebrity who had posed in the nude. The thought of her naked body fills his mind. He tries to bring his imagination back to something wholesome, but the urge to find those pictures just keeps getting stronger.

He decides to get up from his desk and get a cup of coffee. Maybe that will help. He has some time before the other staff comes in to begin their day. He glances down the hall; no one is in yet. His heart begins to race. The thought comes to mind; maybe there will be something on the Internet about the celebrity.

He brings Google up on his computer, selects "images" from the menu bar and types in her name. An hour or so later he is jarred back to reality by the slamming of a car door outside in the parking lot.

He looks at the time and says, "How could I have been looking at all this stuff for over an hour?" What is wrong with me? I've told myself I would never do this again. Oh Lord, please forgive me again? Please help me get free from this! If you don't kill me first, I swear I'll never do this again."

A few hours later, the rest of the staff went out to lunch. Alone in the study with his thoughts, the elder's face comes to mind stinging the pastor again. The elder seemed so angry at him last night at the meeting. The frustration from that encounter bugs him. Then he is overwhelmed by a strong sense of guilt from his lapse in moral judgment earlier that morning. But to his dismay, some of the images he saw on his computer jump back into his head.

He reasons, "Looking never really hurt anyone. Besides, it is secret. It doesn't harm anything. Since I blew it this morning, I guess it doesn't matter now anyway. I wonder if I could find that hot blonde one more time."

The next thing he knows, he is back at the computer screen, fingers typing keywords to new Internet searches. More creative search topics are streaming to his mind and images are appearing on the screen. He'd be ashamed for any of the church people to know what their pastor was doing.

This real-to-life example is a composite of stories I've heard over the years from actual pastors. Part of my own story is woven in there as well. It is essential to identify the subtle patterns of behavior in the story, as well as how quickly we attempt to medicate our emotional pain with some distracting pleasure. Like the picture on the cover of this book, the pastor feels like his hands are dirty, and he doesn't know how to turn them palms up in surrender.

The story I have just told you could just as likely be a businessman and his board of directors. Or it could be a young man who just learned he was being laid off and his home was going into foreclosure. The story could be a spouse who doesn't understand what is happening in his marriage. We can replace the Internet porn, with alcohol, 80-hour work weeks or an affair with the girl or guy in the office. It could be the emotional eater who is 60 pounds overweight and can't stop eating. I could paint scenario after scenario interchanging the destructive tendencies like moving parts . . . But they don't matter.

In every situation there are a few common denominators:

First, there is a situation that creates discomfort and a sense of not knowing what to do.

Next, there is a strong desire to escape the discomfort. This need to avoid the pain is often subconscious, and a person doesn't see how it is related to the hurt or fear buried inside.

Finally, there is a pleasure, escape, and something we would rather feel than the discomfort of the situation. In other words, we work very hard to replace painful conditions with pleasurable sensations.

I've come to believe there is the fourth issue in this pattern. It is an area I was seeking to uncover but just couldn't find. Buried deep within us, at our very core, is an area where we are gravely wounded. It is where hurt, guilt, shame, bitterness and some deeply held false beliefs about ourselves reside.

I believe that core pain and the shame connected to it comes in three realms:

> ➢ The Spiritual Realm
> ➢ The Emotional Realm
> ➢ The Physical Realm

There are also patterns of behavior we have absorbed from childhood. Finally, underneath all the other hurts are some fundamental lies we believe about ourselves. Accepting these false messages ends up driving our unwanted behaviors. Those behaviors reoccur in all adult relationships and like hidden remote controls determine how we respond to spouses, children, and acquaintances.

All the things buried deeply at our core are hidden forces that push and pull us through life often without us even realizing they exist. Those concealed factors influence our choices and behaviors. They sabotage our best efforts to bring change. These core issues are the confounding factors that fuel our most significant battles.

Finally, the unexposed core pain, shame, and beliefs are why most the battles we face are lifelong battles. We patch them with superficial fixes that never deal with the core wound.

I believe Jesus Christ is the Savior of the world, who died to pay for all my sins. I also trust He resurrected from the grave to give me new life and power. I believe He wants me to know what it is to overflow with joy. I believe when I accept Him and His sacrifice for my sins, He forgives me and promises me heaven. This is where I get the courage to invite Him to be my tour guide as I take this hard look inside. Jesus said, "*You are truly my disciples if you stay faithful to my teachings and you will know the truth, and the truth will set you free.*" John 8:31-32. The word, "will" is future tense. Everything I have discovered or that he has revealed to me on my journey is already complete in God's sight. He sees me as the finished product.   He sees me as altogether complete in Jesus Christ. That is the position of all Christians. The problem isn't with my position; it is with my practice!

Behind all behavior is a belief system that drives it. I may believe all the right things about Jesus, but if I don't understand what He says about me, I'm never going to be free. "*And you will know the truth, and the truth will set you free.*"

It is a journey; a process and it takes considerable time and effort. No one, absolutely no one you meet, is whole apart from this process. It is known in theology as sanctification. In everyday language, the sanctification process is the stripping away of all the damaging human traits and beliefs and replacing them with Christ-like qualities. For a clear presentation of how you can begin this process, I would refer you to Appendix A.

The pastor in my earlier story believes everything I just wrote about Jesus, but something deep within drives him to continually sabotage himself. Those who are non-Christians are driven by the same dynamic. I believe no one is exempt. It is the unexamined insides (I'm calling the core in this writing) where all these issues are buried. What happens when people live their lives trying to dodge the truth about these buried matters? The answer is found in

Dr. Keith Ablow's book, <u>Living The Truth</u>. "*It gets harder and harder to stop that truth from surfacing and slapping you hard in the face. You need to find ways to keep your mind from focusing on your pain.*"[1]

At our core then are all these buried wounds that shape our current behaviors. Our past spreads out in front of us and becomes our future mainly because we fear to take the journey to the core facing all those things squarely. We have spent so much energy trying to escape, acting as if those deep wounds never really happened or thinking it was so long ago it does not affect us now. Thus, our core is a buried, locked away, mess of pain, sin, shame, guilt, bitterness and faulty beliefs.

On top of all that, we believe we are unique; no one else could understand. No one else's situation could be like mine. When a person becomes a Christian and is told forgiveness is theirs and now, they have what everyone else needs, it seems like a cruel joke. Instinctively, all of us know we are still not right inside. It seems we are doomed to suffer in silence. One thing we know for sure, if we are the solution to everyone else's problems the world is in big trouble! The pain buried in us is deep and real, and the journey to the core is asking that we stop denying its existence and move toward it rather than away from it, possibly for the first time in our adult lives! It is especially difficult for men because all our culture has ever told us is, "*Big boys don't cry.*" Too much preaching focuses on our position in Christ rather than how to improve our practice, so we stay defeated.

I remember being on the high school wrestling team and breaking my little finger. It shot out perpendicular from my hand. I went to the coach and showed him, and he said, "Here put some tape on it and get back on the mat, you'll be all right." I remember about a year later as a senior in high school playing softball in Phys Ed Class. The same coach fell running to first base and broke his leg. He was on the ground writhing in pain, and I said, "Put a band-aid on it coach, you'll be fine!" He said some things to me at that moment I can't print here!

Men in our culture handle emotional pain just like my coach dealt with physical pain. We try to ignore that it exists. We are not robots! We are not machines. God creates us with emotional capacities that allow us to relate in healthy ways to both God and others. But for men, those painful emotions are bottled up and trapped deep within us. We are clueless as to how to depressurize and release them. More often than not, we are not able to identify or handle our emotional pain, so we suffer in silence; we are angry, isolated and driven.

The more I have learned about the mechanics of all this, the more I've come to believe some of our world's most "successful," individuals are also the least healthy. I watch some professional athletes and their level of drive and know it doesn't come from a healthy place. When the Tiger Woods story broke several years ago, my thought was: If Tiger gets healthy emotionally, he may never attain the same level he had when he was driven.

Healthy people tend to become more balanced. There is not as much need to prove anything, which is one of the side benefits of taking this journey. When there is an apparent success in one part of life while all the rest of your world is in shambles, that isn't a success; that is not healthy. When your career is skyrocketing, but your family life stinks, you are not winning the game! If you are growing a mega-church, but your soul is shrinking, God isn't applauding!

There are so many things buried within us that become the drivers and shapers of the way we live. It is helpful to know what they are so we can make healthier choices. When I watched Brett Favre play football when he was a 41-year-old man, playing injured, and not able to retire; what I saw was an 8 year old boy playing pee-wee football, lying on the ground after getting hurt with his dad as coach standing over him saying, *"Get up boy, Favre's don't get hurt."* I see a man who thinks football is his identity.

Now I don't know that scenario to be accurate, but that would be a clear example of how this dynamic works. Some message we embraced as a child shapes our adult behavior without us even realizing it.

I wonder what voices you hear in your head when you are standing at the edge of a significant opportunity. I wonder if at some fork in the road you experienced something negative and deep down you said, "I will never allow that to happen again."

I wonder what hidden forces, fears or hurts are shaping your life without your comprehension. I wonder what wrong beliefs sabotage you before you start. What do you sense when a strong man or woman issues you an order to do something either at home, work or elsewhere?

I wonder if your life is a boring, routine existence or if it feels more like an exciting adventure being lived out from a confident and quiet strength at your core. As we continue on the journey, the next chapter is going to introduce you to an essential area of understanding you will need to embrace if you plan to complete the journey.

CHAPTER TWO
THE CIRCLE OF
RESPONSIBILITY

After my moral failure in 2000, because I wasn't found out by the congregation, I was able to continue in my role as senior pastor for three and half years. I heard clearly from the Lord that I could not stay at the church, but I couldn't run from it or myself either. My job during my "lame duck" time was to build the church not to need me. I put together a leadership development team who then led our church to build teams that facilitated every facet of the ministry. We also got our facilities and staff in line to carry on after I was gone.

I knew that I heard I would have to leave the church. I had hoped for a full pardon. I had shared the full version of my adultery with Gayle, some counselors and a few close friends early on. But in July of 2004, upon sharing the whole story of my failure, with our elders, I was asked to resign. It was the right decision. Gayle and I sold our home. Our two daughters decided to move to Florida with us. But our son, who was in college and seriously involved with his future bride, stayed behind. During the three years and six-month interim between my failure and my dismissal, I had been humbled, broken and did some major personal development work. I thought I was done with the task of getting healthy. I thought I had gone to the core and cleaned it out. Was I ever mistaken!

The church graciously gave us four months of severance pay for my twelve years of service. That was a grace gift to us that allowed us to move and get settled without worrying about how the bills would be paid. That four months passed quickly, and I soon found out my journey to the core had barely begun.

I went to work as a sales specialist at a big box home improvement store in Brandon, Florida. That experience humbled me to a new level. I was treated like an eighteen-year-old on my first job. No one had any idea who I was the previous eighteen years. No one knew what I had accomplished in life, and no one cared. The weight of what I lost came crashing down on me.

I began to despise life. Many evenings I would sit in my Jeep Wrangler during my supper break by myself eating the lunch Gayle packed for me. I would watch the sunset silhouetting the palm trees in the beauty of Florida, where I now lived. I was never more lonely, miserable and disconnected in my life. After my hour of rehashing my loss, I'd trudge back in the store and work until 10 or 11 p.m. I've always hated being away from home during those evening hours. The most profound loneliness I've ever known came over me during those times.

All this time, Gayle loved Florida. We have a beautiful home, swimming pool, etc. The climate here is so lovely; she loved everything about her new life out of the fishbowl. As I had lost my identity, she was finding hers. I hated not being in the middle of everything; she loved being out of public life. It irritated me that Gayle was so contented here and I was so miserable. Neither of us at this point could enter into the world of the other.

I believed if somehow, I could get back in ministry as a pastor again I'd be happy. Gayle would say, "You weren't happy as a pastor before, why do you think it would be different now?" I wanted to move back home to Chesapeake, Virginia. I thought I wanted to move all the way back home to Williamsport, Pennsylvania. I was so unhappy with my life, and it seemed like there was nothing I could do about any of it. I felt trapped in a snare of my own making.

During this time, I went through a whole group of life changes. It seemed the Lord was showing me the things that I thought would make me happy weren't what I needed. My job was brutal. It was my first retail experience at a big box store. Our store did a million dollars of business per week. We were severely understaffed. Weekends were like feeding frenzies with twenty customers for every red-vested employee, and they all wanted something at once.

The customers were often angry at our inability to keep up with their demands. I regularly heard threats that they were going to our competitor across town! I started telling people we had a shuttle bus to the competitor's store out front and it left every twenty minutes. They may want to get on the next one! The expectations of us were impossible to meet. The style of management at our store seemed more like military boot camp. It was designed to break you. I came to believe if you survived, they made you a manager! If you quit, they would hire more cheap help.

I was required to work 50 hours a week minimum at the time. Life was turned on end for me, and I didn't like it. I only could go to church once a month, and honestly, that was once a month too often! When I went to church, all I felt was how superficial it all was. The frustrations, anger, discontentment had grown so much that I was angry at God, my job, Gayle, church and pretty much the world. I honestly was waiting for somebody to push the wrong button at the wrong time and as a former wrestler and amateur boxer, there was going to be an explosion of fury taken out on somebody's head. I told Gayle one time; I feel sorry for whomever it is that pushes that last button because when I unleash the fury, it won't be pretty.

I felt that most of my frustration came from my job so I said, "Lord, this job is unbearable, can't you do any better than this for someone who gave so much to you?" Within a brief period, we had a man come to our home study group from church, who invited me to breakfast. He told me he knew I was frustrated with my job and he needed to hire someone for the company where he worked. He ended up hiring me.

I had worked the retail job for one full year - A year of purgatory. I was finally free to enter a career that would turn out to suit my personality and gifts perfectly. The pay and benefits were more than I expected. No more weekend work. I was able to work from a home office. The position gave me much freedom and very little stress. I honestly had no idea there was a position like this anywhere in the world. As bad as my year of retail was for me, this career with a natural gas utility was at the other end of the spectrum. My work life was now excellent! But I was coming to realize my frustration wasn't my job. I was still discontented with much of my life.

One-night Gayle and I went for a walk, and I told her about how frustrated I had become. I felt we didn't have enough disposable income. Nor did I have an outlet for ministry. As it turned out, the next night I went to a men's group at our church. The meeting was okay, but from my experience, I knew it needed something more. About a week later the pastor, who was leading the men's group, asked me if I would be willing to take over. I was thrilled with the prospect of being involved with the team at a leadership level. It was encouraging to discover it would be a paid part-time position.

I took the position, and in an instant, I had two of my most pressing frustrations resolved: Gayle and I had some extra income; and, I now had a new ministry opportunity. The Lord had stepped in and met my needs with one solution. I see now; He was showing me these external issues were not really what was causing my discontentment. Despite all the Lord had done for us, I still had a high degree of agitation in my spirit.

I am a runner. For those who know me, they understand how important running is to me, both on a fitness and spiritual level. Almost everything I am putting into this book is a result of answers and thoughts that have come to me while I was running. I do a lot of talking to the Lord and an equal amount of listening on my early morning runs.

I run five miles, several times each week. I rarely miss an opportunity to head out in the cool of the morning. My most significant motivation at this point is the hope of an encounter with the Lord. Those runs are where I pour out my innermost thoughts to Him, and He talks back to me. On my runs, I've cried, been angry, preached sermons, pleaded, questioned and have gained many insights through this time with God. Honestly, the physical benefits pale compared to the spiritual benefits I gain from running.

So, one morning I was running, and I'm pouring out my heart to God. "I feel like you are punishing me, Lord, you've taken me from being the senior pastor of a growing church and stuck me in a part-time ministry in a back room with a handful of guys. I've confessed everything to you and those I've hurt; I've repented so why are you still punishing me? What is wrong, are you embarrassed by me God? Do you think I'm going to screw up again and you can't trust me with more? Can we just move? I want to go home! I'm not happy here, and I'm angry that Gayle is!"

When I could calm down a little and just be silent again, I waited for an answer. I'm amazed at the patience of God in this journey. When I was done blowing off steam, he gave me one of the most valuable lessons I have ever received.

I sensed the Lord beginning to instruct me, "Son, I want you to picture a circle in your mind."

I said, "Okay, I've got it."

The teaching continued, "Now draw a stick figure inside your circle."

"Got it again," I said.

Here is what I pictured in its simplicity.

His instruction became personal now. "Son, if the person inside this circle is miserable; if this person is not filled with love, joy and peace, and the fruit of my spirit. who do you think should be held responsible?" There was a pause as I contemplated His question. "Everything outside the circle will have an impact on the person inside the circle. Outside the circle are other people's actions and words and personal agendas."

"If you haven't figured it out yet son, YOU are the person inside the circle. You are only responsible for responding in a manner that would honor me. Do you recall my words? 'One day you will stand before me and give an account of YOURSELF to me.' (Romans 14:12). So, why do you keep blaming everything and everyone outside your circle for what is wrong inside your circle?"

What I was beginning to see, was that I was the biggest problem I have! I **_am_** my own worst enemy! I now understood it would be my responsibility to figure out why I was so miserable. I knew blaming anything outside my circle was not going to be an acceptable answer. So, I needed to continue looking at things within the circle, within my ability to change. For me, this was an epiphany, but for others, well, I believe they had figured this part out long ago, "God grant me the serenity . . ."[2]

To give you a better understanding of the concept of living inside the circle, I want to take you back and revisit the pastor who is looking at pornography in his office to medicate the frustration and anger he was feeling towards the problematic and combative elder. I've come to understand that much of our ability to handle life more healthily involves telling the truth motivated by love.

My inability to be honest about my thoughts and feelings toward others (to please them) has caused much of the frustration in my life. I struggled for years with this: attempting to lead a church with people on a governing board who were apparently coming from a different philosophy of ministry. It created constant friction, frustration and lack of progress. No wonder I was so miserable & experienced failure leading!

I endured this never clearly stating what I felt or leading to remedy the problem. I blamed the elder who opposed me at every turn, talked *about* him but not *to* him. I medicated my hurts in numerous ways. I viewed *him* as the problem, never acknowledging that I could be contributing to the problem.

The entire time the answer was within my ability to solve. It was in my circle. I now understand this simple concept: I was the senior leader, and there was disharmony in my leadership team. Part of my team was committed to a traditional style of ministry, and the remainder was committed to a contemporary model. It was my responsibility to correct the issue. It was my responsibility to 'train others or be traded myself.'

The proper approach was to open a dialogue. In a perfect world, the team would come to a consensus about the direction. In the real world, every leader around the table had their issues: wounds, fears, motives and protective layers. The problem was mine to solve. My approach revealed my lack of leadership skills, but also highlighted the solution: if I could gain control of my part, it would make a difference. And that is what I did.

In a meeting, putting the wellbeing of the ministry ahead of my comfort, I told the truth in love. I said, "I can no longer lead with a group of people who are going in opposite directions."

The contentious elder who was always opposing my plans spoke up. He asked, "What are you talking about?" I was direct in my response. I said, "You oppose everything I have suggested. You have told us all before you felt I was trying to lead the church in a direction that was far away from what we used to be. So, let me make this clear: I am not looking for 'yes men,' I am asking for a team – this team, to all, be pulling in the same direction."

In ministry, pulling in the same direction means everyone has the same underlying philosophy of how the leadership team will operate. There is a mutual respect for each member, but often there will be very intense and animated discussions as to the practical application of the plan.

When philosophies are different, it is like chaining vehicles together, pointing in opposite directions and expecting them to drive to the same place. It is the pushing and pulling that impedes the forward progress. That was how our elder board had become over the previous couple years. We had stalled.

One example comes to mind: We changed the church name, dropping the denominational label. Our purpose was to make the church more appealing to a broader community of people who had either no religious background or a different one. But our church sign, which was twenty feet tall, still had the denominational name on it. Every time I brought up the fact that "it did no good to change our name on paper while the well-lit sign everyone driving by was able to see, still had the old name on it," it fell on deaf ears.

He had opposed my suggestion because he wanted the church to stay just the way it always was. He would make a formal motion to table the issue for further study. Sometimes his reasons bordered on the bizarre. One time he stated: "We should see if spotlights shining on the sign would be better than the internal lighting." It just made no sense. It was apparent to all the men on the leadership team that he was only stalling. This issue was consistently tabled for over a year.

So, I finally took responsibility for what was 'inside my circle.' I went to this brother and told the truth in love. By doing so, I uncovered his real agenda and gave him an opportunity to serve in some other capacity. It was amazing how quickly a sense of love, peace, and cooperation returned to our leadership team.

You see, this elder should have been in a traditional church where he would have been comfortable. The entire time the solution to this problem was inside my circle of responsibility! The elder's philosophy of ministry (his agenda) was outside my circle, but the responsibility of oversight for our leadership team and its productivity was wholly mine. As soon as I took responsibility for my part, I was able to solve the problem.

But understanding the circle of responsibility didn't fix me; it didn't heal what was broken inside of me. What this insight did, however, was to move squarely onto my shoulders, the responsibility for doing the hard and necessary work to begin to figure myself out. There is a slogan familiar in circles of people who are doing this kind of introspective work on themselves. It goes like this, "No matter where I go, there I am." If I'm miserable with my life in Florida, I would still be unhappy with my life if I were to move to Virginia, Pennsylvania or Mars!

The Lord is using the concept of the "*circle of responsibility*" in many ways and areas of my life. It has helped the lives of the men that I teach as well. The guys have talked about making T-shirts with the man in the circle on them. One man said, he drew the circled stick figure on a piece of paper, printed it out and posted it in his cubicle at work. He uses it as a reminder to himself that he and he alone is responsible for what is inside his circle. Many times, in my work situations I to have drawn the little man in a circle at the top of the paper as a reminder to take care of myself and my responsibilities. The circle drawing always leads me to ask the question, what is my part in this situation.

It is critical early in this journey; we all come to terms with this apparent fact. You and I are entirely responsible for our journey. I am accountable for my journey to the core and any resulting happiness. If I am not a happy camper, there is no one else in the tent to blame, and the location of the campsite makes no difference. It is my responsibility, and I will one day give an account of how I handled my life and its tests.

If you can accept the truth of this chapter; when you can say the happiness you long for is within your power to attain; when you can take full responsibility without laying blame on anyone else for your discontentment - then you are ready to proceed on the journey to the core.

In the next chapter, I'm going to begin uncovering what the 'feared' core contains. You may be surprised at what I discovered deep within myself as I ventured into what I will define as the three realms of buried pain.

CHAPTER THREE
THREE REALMS OF
BURIED PAIN

I n the early days of my discovery, I believed the symptoms of the struggle were the struggle itself. What I mean by that is, the person who has a drinking or drug problem often feels if they could just give up the bad behavior, they would be fine. The person who battles obesity thinks, *"I'd be okay if I could just lose this excess weight."* Thousands of Christian men believe life would be great if they could give up their porn habit. The truth is there is good news and bad news.

As we will discover in the next several chapters, those habits or addictions only mask the real issues of our lives. The good news is you don't have to abuse drugs, drink to excess, emotionally over-eat, and spend even a moment viewing porn or any other escapist behavior. The bad news is, these things are not the real problem.

The real issues are so woven into the fabric of our lives that we are blind to them. They drive our behaviors. They have damaged our past, cripple us in the present and sabotage our futures. We are oblivious to them. It is as if we are fighting with an invisible opponent. Let's begin to examine the three realms of buried pain.

The first realm is **spiritual**. Like it or not, believe it or not, we are spiritual beings. Innately, we know there is a God. It matters little if you have ever gone to church or read the Bible. The truth is *"The heavens declare the glory of God and all the people see His glory."* Psalm 97:6. Also, these verses tell a powerful story, *"For ever since the world was created, people have seen the earth and sky. Through everything God made, they can clearly see his invisible qualities—his eternal power and divine nature. So, they have no excuse for not knowing God. Yes, they knew God, but they wouldn't worship him as God or even give him thanks. And they began to think up foolish ideas of what God was like. As a result, their minds became dark and confused. Claiming to be wise, they instead became utter fools."* (Romans 1:20-22).

I remember even as a little boy having a sense there was a God. I also had a very acute awareness of guilt when I did something wrong. It was internal. I had trouble sleeping at night if I did something wrong until I would tell my mom. The relief of confession was immediate, and I could sleep. Apparently, I was a slow learner because as I got older, I learned to bury guilt feelings rather than confess them. As my behaviors became more reckless, daring and dirty, the guilt and shame had to be suppressed for me to function. Though I knew I had done many things wrong, ultimately, my judgment of myself was that I was better than average. I was sure God liked me and would let me come to heaven when I died. I continued to live however I pleased, sowing my wild oats and praying for crop failure.

I want all Christian readers to sit up and listen carefully to this part. At twenty-one years of age, my sin had begun to catch up with me. Gayle and I had already been married two years and had a one-year-old daughter. By this point, I was living a life of my choosing. My moral compass wasn't functioning correctly, and I did pretty much as I pleased.

The consequences and repercussions of the way I was living were about to come home to roost. Our marriage was on the rocks; I was in deep trouble. Gayle and I began going to church at the invitation of a relative. I heard the good news that Jesus Christ died on a cross to pay for all my sin. I was taught He also rose from the grave. This double barrel blast, his death for my sin and his resurrection to give new life, was my ticket. I embraced the message to the best of my ability. I believe the gospel of Jesus Christ is God's power to save all who will believe (Romans 1:16). Our spiritual dilemma is not a negative reflection on the gospel's power to save. It is, however, a negative reflection on our understanding of how deeply the sin issue goes. Preachers tell us to confess our sin; some may even say confess we are sinners. What exactly does that mean?

When I accepted Christ as a twenty-one-year-old, on my knees by my bed, all I confessed was "sinful acts and attitudes." I had no clue how deeply my sinful nature goes and what untruths it tells me.

Some of the responsibility for this superficial belief lies in the American Church and her leadership. Our pastors don't know what they don't know. There is a total disregard among most for the depth of this buried pain and the lies that fuel us. There also seems to be an underlying ignorance of anything except for this spiritual realm. I have never heard in any church about the next two realms of buried pain I will uncover. The amazing thing now that I see this truth, it has always been in Scripture. I comprehend how God desires for us to take this journey all the way to the source. Consider this bible verse, "*For the word of God is alive and powerful. It is sharper than the sharpest two-edged sword, cutting between soul and spirit, between joint and marrow. It exposes our innermost thoughts and desires. [13] Nothing in all creation is hidden from God. Everything is naked and exposed before his eyes, and he is the one to whom we are accountable.*" (Hebrews 4:12-13).

I've come to see that until my core was discovered, healed and redeemed, my ministry would come from some protective layer on the surface. We will learn more thoroughly about these protective layers later.

Evidence of ministering from a superficial layer appears when I offer bible quotes as solutions to everything instead of the compassion and love of Christ from my heart. Instead of weeping with those who weep and celebrating with those who celebrate I offer pious platitudes or try to celebrate while being envious inside. It is interesting that the two key leaders of the early church had been broken before Christ used them powerfully. Peter was humbled and broken by his denial of Christ. Paul was pulverized through his Damascus Road experience. Paul's experience was so humbling that he said, the religious layer he had fabricated, he now counts as dung! (Philippians 3:7-8)

The buried pain God has revealed to me in the spiritual realm is a sense of shame and guilt, not for anything I've done, but just because I'm me. There are genuinely held wrong beliefs I will unpack later. Keep in mind; this is what I've discovered at my core even as a believer in Jesus Christ. The reason the faulty beliefs could remain intact is they are so woven into the fabric of who I am; I never knew they were there! Now that I see it, I also see how much that buried pain dominated my behavior. Those core misbeliefs affect every interaction with other people. This isn't just low self-esteem! This is an accumulation of messages we have heard from others growing up and stories we have told ourselves when we fail.

It is interesting the scriptures teach the enemy wants to destroy our lives and one of his tactics is to blind our minds so the healing power of the gospel cannot penetrate to these deep recesses. (2 Corinthians 4:3-4). My purpose at this point is not to give you remedies; it is to help you see what is at the root of your behaviors. Our aim to allow the truth to penetrate all the outer layers and cut deeply to the "thoughts and intents" of your heart. The solutions come a bit later. The painful words and experience connected to this discovery are I am unlovable, I am shame-filled, and I am guilt-ridden.

The second realm of buried pain I've discovered is **emotional**. Spiritual and emotional pain is similar but different. The spiritual is how we understand our relationship or lack thereof with God. I believe the one word that most would use to describe what they feel when they think about God is guilt. Emotional pain is more human. It is based on our deepest beliefs about how others view us or how we perceive they would see us if they knew us. The understanding of this realm is mostly absent from Christian circles. It is very prevalent in treatment programs that help people with addictions. I previously believed this one area was the fuel for almost all addictive behaviors. I've come to think that addictions are fueled by all three realms of buried pain and our inability to handle hurt. Most in recovery have heard they are dealing with a three-headed monster, spiritual, emotional and physical and that is true.

Getting to the core pain in this area required me to look hard at my family dynamic. This part could be painful for some of my family members to read, but it is my perspective. First, a disclaimer must be given. I believe no parent can give what they don't have. All of us do the best we can with what we have at the time. My three children could take this journey and find things I didn't do very well as a dad that caused them hurt. That is the nature of life on a fallen planet. I believe both parents loved me to the best of their ability. My parents remained married for 42 years until my dad's passing. I grew up in a stable environment healthier than many. The level of buried pain in the emotional realm could be almost unbearable for some less fortunate. Because each of us is responsible for our own lives within our circle, there are no excuses, no blaming of others that will stand. No blaming allowed. Before I get to my story, I want to share someone else's story of taking responsibility and turning negatives into positives.

I recently heard Liz Murray tell her story. She is the author of the New York Times Bestseller *"Breaking Night,"* and the subject of the Lifetime Network's original film, *"Homeless to Harvard: The Liz Murray Story."* Liz grew up in squalor with addicted parents in the Bronx. It was a brutal existence. She was often homeless, unschooled and uncared for. But she believed the truth about the circle of responsibility. At seventeen years of age, she woke up to the realization no one was going to make her way in life but her. As a homeless teen, she finally found a high school that would allow her to attend. She crammed four years of high school into two and graduated as a straight "A" student.

She heard about a grant provided for a needy student to pay for college offered by the New York Times. To be considered you had to write your hardship story and why you needed help. Liz wrote her story, and the rest is history. She won the award and graduated from Harvard with a degree in Psychology.

Along the way, Oprah caught wind of her story, the Lifetime Network after that. Liz now is one of the most sought-after inspirational speakers in the world, drawing six figures for her talks.[3]

Your story and my story are probably like fairy tales compared to Liz's, but understanding the dynamics of your home life is crucial to finding the buried pain in the emotional realm. What I did was considered all the possible traits for each parent. I made a sheet with two columns and put "mom" on one side and "dad" on the other. Under each, I listed the options. I considered things like personality features, what their home life was like, their dominant traits as I perceived them. Fortunately, for me, my grandparents on both sides lived long enough for me to have a good understanding of the family dynamics that shaped my parents as well.

This part of my story is intensely personal. I always knew I was loved, especially by my mom. I was her favorite. I knew it because she told me. My brother and sister would readily say they felt that was true. One time when I was little, mom was sick and stayed in bed. I made her scrambled eggs, toast and hot tea and served her in bed. She said, *"Don't tell the other kids but you are my best kid."* Mom and I have always been close; in fact, we've discussed all that I'm writing here.

Now let's fast forward years and years ahead to the present. I woke up one night out of a sound sleep and sat right up in bed. I got up and wrote a full page about favoritism. What hit me is this; favoritism has little to do with the child shown favor and everything to do with the parent showing favor. When this truth hit me, I called mom. I asked her to describe her relationship with her mom.

I discovered that though she had five brothers all but one older than her, mom would often be put in charge of all the kids when her parents went away. I asked, *"Doesn't it seem strange to you in that day, a young girl with four older brothers would be put in charge?"* Mom said, *"It was because I was most responsible."* Instantly, my perception was mom did whatever it took to make her mom happy, just like I did with her. I needed my mother's affirmation and approval so much I was willing to give up myself to keep her happy. The result was I was shown favor.

That is not loving at the highest level. Love at the purest level is I do for you with no expectation of return. In true love, my action is to benefit you not for personal gain. I started to realize that if I stopped working so hard to stay in mom's orbit, I could be demoted to the *"shit-list,"* quite quickly. I saw this conditioned type of love when I lost my position as a pastor through my moral failure. It is as if, mom refuses to acknowledge that loss. For her to tell the truth by saying her son lost his ministry due to his moral failure would produce shame. That is understandable and her issue. From my vantage point, I saw my failure brought shame rather than pride. So, for years, even though I was no longer in ministry, mom introduced me to people as her pastor son. My core discovery in the emotional realm then is this. I am only lovable when I can perform and produce in a way that makes someone else proud of me or in some way enhances their image.

This pattern uncovered and unrecognized programmed me to become a people pleaser. If Gayle was happy, I must be doing well. If she looked upset, I figured I did something wrong. If the church leaders had a burr under their saddle, it became my problem to attempt to make them happy again. I was driven by this need to earn people's love and affection. I never believed someone could love me just for me; I always had to perform to their liking.

I was also thinking through what I absorbed about being a man through my boyhood environment. Mom is a dominant personality, very gregarious and somewhat controlling. My dad was a deep thinker, reserved, appeared disengaged emotionally and was passive at home. In my quest to figure out the forces at work deep within, I typed in Google, *"domineering mom passive dad."*

I was blown away by what I discovered. It was like finding and reading my secret journal. It said boys growing up in this environment might lead in every other realm of their lives, but when they come home, they disengage and passively resist their wives.

I started thinking about times my family would all be together, and the kids would say, *"Dad, why don't you join us instead of being on the computer."* They would ask, *"Dad, do you want to play a game or do something besides watching TV?"* Gayle has asked me often over the years, *"Why is it anytime I make a suggestion you get angry?"* It was like reading that article on *"Passivity in Men,"*[4] opened my eyes to see this pattern. I came to terms with this as a learned behavior. I had absorbed this and just felt it was typical for men.

This passivity has far-reaching implications. It has caused me to think someone owes me something. Rather than initiating things with Gayle, I wait for her to make a plan. But then I don't like her idea. I'm waiting for life to be delivered on a silver platter. I expect other people to make decisions for me that are mine to make. Rather than going after a promotion, I get upset when my employer doesn't come to me and offer me a promotion. Rather than express my interest in an opportunity at church, I get upset the opportunity isn't brought to me.

This passivity is a source of buried frustration and pain at the core of my life. It has created much anger and bitterness over the years that I just stuff down because of my people pleasing tendencies. These two forces together, people pleasing and passivity, create a toxic brew! So, what I discovered at the core in the emotional realm is the sense I'm not lovable unless I please you and I am not adequate to actively engage in life. The emotional terms and experiences connected to this discovery are I feel shame, resentment, and bitterness; I express anger, frustration, and unhappiness.

The final realm of buried pain is **physical**. We live in a time when physical and verbal abuse is prevalent. This buried pain may be created by actual physical pain or the messages we have heard, or the stories we have believed about our physical bodies and appearance. I've never met anyone who said, *"I am just totally content with everything about me, I wouldn't change anything even if I could."* Rather, all of us think, *"If only I were. . ."* I wish I was 6' 4" and was a super athlete. I wish my hair were a different color. I wish my nose weren't so big.

According to data from a USA Today article from April 12, 2017, Americans have spent 6 billion dollars in 2016 on plastic surgery with breast implants and nose jobs leading the way.[5] It is clear; we are not happy with the way we look. For some, childhood teasing, rejection by peers and being dismissed as undesirable because of some physical flaw can create shame or embarrassment. It ties deeply with the emotional level because of the lies we believe. It is a lie to think if we looked a certain way, we would be more deserving of love and acceptance. If you suffered physical abuse, the physical pain fades, but the emotional wounding remains until you do some hard work to uncover and heal the wounds.

I remember being teased because of some physical attributes as a kid. One that stands out to me is I have always been short. I'm 5' 7 1/2," but I say I'm 5' 8". Growing up I was always the smallest kid on baseball teams. They used to line us up by size and give out uniforms numbered from one to fifteen. I always wore number 1! In high school wrestling back in the 1970's the lowest weight class was 95 lbs. Many schools forfeited that weight because they didn't have any sophomores that small. Our school had forfeited that weight for years. Our coach was thrilled when I came to high school because I only weighed 92 lbs.! I had played sports up till I was twelve years old. I excelled at baseball and football. I was super-fast, played quarterback and running back on my Pop Warner Football Teams. In Little League Baseball led the entire league in stolen bases, had the highest batting average on our team, played shortstop and pitched. Then everyone else grew, and I didn't. I started wrestling but didn't like it. It was about the only sport I could compete in because I was so small and wrestling has weight divisions. My dad used to say, *"Dynamite comes in a small package."* I don't think I believed him!

It hurts anytime we hear negative messages about the way we are physically. To hear girls, say, *"He is too short."* To hear the tone in someone's voice when they say, *"How much do you weigh?"* I wanted to go out for the high school football team my first year. I went to the coach and said, *"I want to play football. I was very good at the lower levels and thought with my speed I could still contribute."* He looked at me and said, *"How much do you weigh boy?"* Even though I weighed about 90 lbs. on a good day; I said, *"About a hundred pounds,"* he burst out laughing and said, *"Wet or dry?"* Now, even at my age and place in life to hear or read about people saying, *"I would never date a man who is only 5'8","* stings a little. I catch myself wondering what if? What if I had the same level of athleticism, I have but had the body of a Tim Tebow?

I can only imagine what could be locked up down deep in this physical realm if someone had a severe disability or disfigurement. What if someone was teased relentlessly as a child because of how he or she looked? The wounds can be profound and super painful. When people make light of us based on these things, it creates a sense of shame, humiliation, and inadequacy.

So, buried deeply at the core of who I am I discovered these three realms of hidden pain. I don't like pain, and that is why I was content to allow it to stay buried for so long. What began to come to me from the abyss of denial is the realization that behind all three realms of pain were the same fundamental lies. So many of us, just want to move forward and never look back, never look deeply within. Rather than take the journey to the core, we wrap the core with protective layers. The next chapter is going to examine three layers of protection I've discovered I used to protect that buried pain.

CHAPTER FOUR
THREE LAYERS OF PROTECTION

Everything within us is programmed to run away from pain. We hate pain! One early morning on my run I was thinking about all the things I wrote in Chapter Three. I got a mental picture of a vast dark circle representing the core. The core had a set of double doors that could be opened. I pictured Gayle and me as little children holding hands and timidly opening those doors. Inside the doors was a raging blast furnace, much like the three Hebrew children were thrown into as recorded in Daniel 3. They were tied up and thrown into the furnace that had been heated to seven times its normal temperature.

Often, our stories are very similar. We are only willing to do the hard work of this journey to the core when life forces us. We wait until we are thrown into the furnace of our wounded cores. Until that happens, all humans take an alternative course of action. We build protective layers around our core pain and run away from it as fast as we can and hope it will just disappear. As I worked my way toward the center of my being, I discovered three layers that I had built up to protect myself. Those three segments are religious, social and secret.

True spirituality requires humility, openness, and honesty. Religion, on the other hand, is a disguise to prop us up in the eyes of other people. True spirituality works hard on personal development while giving others grace to work on their progress. Religion tends to judge others on specific criteria that will make the practitioner appear to be superior. Spirituality focuses on one's connection to God and sharing his love and blessing with others. Religion often focuses on the failures and lacks of others and adds more demands. Religion works hard to hide personal failures; spirituality uses failure and redemption as the platform for growth and ministry.

Often this **religious** layer creates a person that seems to say all the right things and knows what it takes to be in the Christian club. The problem is their attitudes often betray them. Their relationships usually are strained. The expectations of others are unrealistic and drive people away. The last things they would ever be accused of is being joy-filled and winsome.

I recently heard a radio interview with a lady who was infertile. She was discussing the pain and frustration with not being able to conceive. She said the Christians who were the least help were those who came to her and said, "*Now you know all things work together for good. God has a plan.*" The lady also said the people who were the most comforting to her were the ones who would listen to her vent. The friends who would hold her hand and cry with her; who would just stay by her side in the darkest times while offering no solutions. When we offer simple religious solutions and expect people to shape up, it shows a great misunderstanding of the human condition and places undue stress on the struggler.

Jesus talked about this to the religious people of his day when he said you place demands on men's shoulders but you don't lift a finger to keep them yourself. The religious protective layer is all about keeping everyone else at arm's length so they can never discover who we are. The religious layer is an embellishment built out of the fear of rejection.

I had fabricated this layer in my life as soon as I started regularly attending church. I had become a Christian. Every message I heard was about what Christians were supposed to do and not do. I never heard anyone in our church admit to doing anything on the *"Don't do list."* The only exception to that was a girl who got pregnant before marriage. The church forced the guy and girl to confess to the entire church family. There were embarrassment and shame for the family. No wonder no one ever admitted to anything wrong at church!

Early in my Christian experience, though I wanted to please the Lord and do the right things the buried core of pain fueled behaviors that were not acceptable. I felt at the time; I had no other recourse than to build a superficial religious veneer that said and did all the right things while burying all failures, shame, and guilt where they could never be discovered. Don't make me too much of a villain here. Part of me wanted to love the Lord with all my heart. I wanted to please Him as much as I wanted to please my mom growing up. I would confess to Him when I sinned. At the same time, all the buried pain was like a hidden driver that pushed and pulled me to a variety of ways to kill the pain.

Read Romans chapter seven in the Bible and see if it doesn't parallel my experience. Without realizing it, I did things to build these protective layers that added more shame and guilt to the core wound. What I mean by that is anytime we pretend to be something we know we are not, it just brings more condemnation. What I assumed was my protection added to my undoing.

At the same time, I was hammered continuously with the message that I was to tell others about Jesus. I was to be a missionary, and the rest of the world was the mission field. I'm supposed to help others understand this message I was given so they could be "like us." No wonder the church gurus estimate that only 3-5 people in a congregation of 200 ever share their faith! The Christian Community has blunted the tip of the two-edged sword by our lack of understanding. We expect people who know they are messed up to tell others how to be healthy. Physician heal yourself!

My inability to tell the truth for fear of having someone angry with me caused me much anguish as a pastor. I felt I had to keep everyone happy. I did all the check boxes of the church, read my Bible, prayed, conducted services, and gave money, etc. But I also had a growing discontentment, anger and desire to escape while pretending everything was okay.

My religious protective layer grew thicker with time. The higher I rose in Christian circles the more hypocritical I became. I held an orthodox belief system, I could preach to others, and I could lead a ministry. I could counsel others about their problems and had some excellent insights because of my struggles. I could share with others about failures that happened ten years ago but never one that occurred last week. I had nowhere to go with any current struggle for fear of losing my job.

This religious layer is one of the most common. Here is the evidence. More people talk about their faith than practice it. This type of religion is useless, powerless and cannot free us from anything. Almost everyone can spot a hypocrite, and nobody likes them. There is some hypocrisy in us all.

There is much in Scripture about this religious layer. Look at the Pharisees in the New Testament.[6] But one of the most visible examples of this is the Apostle Paul. Read Philippians 3 and look at the elaborate religious layer he had constructed during his days in Judaism.[7] Paul was so proud of his accomplishments and lists all of them. But when he had a real encounter with the resurrected Christ his whole religious layer was demolished. It was replaced by a humility that said, *"For me to live is Christ; I've given up everything so I could know Him."*[8]

I also discovered there is a **<u>social</u>** layer of protection. This is being pushed more and more by the concept of political correctness. The social layer of protection is I do what I have to do to be accepted and to keep you away from who I am at the core. Once I was no longer in the professional ministry world and was a Christian in the marketplace, I noticed this protective layer more than before. In my mind, I wasn't an official representative of Christianity any longer. It wasn't as important that I engage in conversations that previously I would have eagerly voiced my convictions. I was in a new world, trying to make my way. That world would require a stronger social veneer if I were to fit in.

I found a great social protective layer story in the Bible. In John 4, Jesus encounters the Samaritan woman at the well. Samaritans were multi-ethnic Jews and despised in that day. Also, women in that culture were viewed mainly as possessions. A woman could not divorce a man. Her whole place in society was based on having a man provide for her, protect her and to bear children. A man could divorce a woman for any reason. To be divorced by a man meant you were not good enough. A woman was in a very vulnerable place in society to be left on her own. Read the story of Ruth to get a sense of this truth.

So, Jesus encounters this woman at the well in the middle of the day. She was drawing water for some animals. The woman was totally dumbfounded that Jesus would talk to her. Here is a woman who has never met a man who didn't have some selfish use for her. There was something about Jesus; he leaked the love and grace of God. He said, *"Go call your husband."* She gave her socially protective layer answer, *"I have no husband."* She was presenting an image of herself that was better than the truth. That is what this social layer does. The truth is shame-filled, painful and degrading, thus avoided. Jesus' gospel was not content to only penetrate a superficial layer he goes right to the core. *"You told me the truth; you have no husband because you have had five husbands and the man you are living with now is not your husband."*[9] I believe Jesus said this with compassion in his eyes; he met her at the core level of her pain and didn't condemn her. He loved her, and she felt it. She was humiliated to say I've had five men who believed I wasn't lovable; I wasn't good enough. The guy I live with now is afraid to take a chance, and I'm so desperate I'm willing to sell myself cheap just to have a place to live. Thus, her safe answer was, I don't have a husband. See how this social protection works? We present ourselves in a way that makes us appear better than we feel we are.

I have found the layers of protection build a fictitious person, a straw man that is opposite of all the things we believe about ourselves. I had confused what I did with who I was so much that not being a pastor was extremely difficult. I didn't know what to do. I didn't know how to present myself to new people I met. Especially while wearing my Lowes vest. Since the time I was twenty-five years old, I was either preparing to be a pastor or was a pastor. Now at fifty years of age, I found myself softening why I was no longer a pastor when explaining it to others.

I regularly heard myself say *"I was a senior pastor for eighteen years. Yeah, I turned fifty, and my wife and I decided we'd had enough and decided to move to Florida."* I told the story in a way that made me appear better than I was. Living from that social layer of protection nullifies reality. Life from that level is fiction. I've come to believe I am not ready to live till I can live from a healthy core, till I can face the demands of reality. When what we think about ourselves is too much to bear, the shame of what we are can no longer maintain the facade. We must take stronger and stronger measures.

It reminds me of the story of Mark Madoff, on the second anniversary of his father's arrest for the famous Ponzi scheme,

Mark hung himself in his apartment with a dog leash. The shame and embarrassment were more than he could endure. By the time someone reaches the point of suicide they have already built a robust third layer.

The **secret** protective layer is built to numb the pain we cannot bear. Our core wound is so powerful, the emotion so strong we can no longer avoid it with our religious and social pretense. The accusing voices, the feelings of shame, embarrassment, failure, bitterness, and fear have to be silenced. Our inner voice calls us out as imposters, and it needs to be deadened. The things we do at this level would not be socially acceptable to our peers. That is why it is a secret layer. This is the layer of addictive behaviors, drugs, alcohol, sex, porn, emotional eating, and workaholism.

Often this layer involves overt sin; the first two layers contain a subtler type of unhealthy living. Most churches rarely touch this third level except to condemn the behaviors. *The problem is most struggling with this secret level believe these practices are their core problem.* That just is not true. All these actions are symptoms of deeper levels of pain. These acts also contribute to the shame and guilt that accumulates at the core. *"And this is the message I proclaim—that the day is coming when God, through Christ Jesus, will judge everyone's secret life"* Romans 2:16.

For a Christian person, the exposure of this secret layer, usually by having it exposed by others, will become the motivation to begin the journey to their core issues. The humbling and brokenness that comes from their public humiliation is enough pain to push them into the path of healing. Not until the pain of the struggle is more significant than the pleasure of the escape will a person seek help. One of my goals is through sharing my journey others will join me before they are crushed!

Now that we have examined the spiritual, emotional and physical things that contribute to our core pain. And, now that we have considered the three protective layers, we construct including religious, social and secret layers. We are going to look right into the blast furnace of our core and discover the deep core lies we believe that fuel our unhealthy behaviors.

CHAPTER FIVE
CORE LIE ONE
I AM NOT LOVEABLE

God intended for us to know and live in his great love. The enemy was partially correct when he whispered into the ear of our first parents, *"God knows when you eat this, you will become like God.*[10]*"* Previously, they knew they were loved by their creator. After the fall every human being has been born believing an evil lie, *"I am not lovable."* There is a variation of this lie that says, *"I will be loved by you if."*

The latter lie is what fuels peer pressure and our performance-based culture. We have three significant enemies in our lives. The Bible calls those three, Satan, the world system, and our sinful human nature. The three work in harmony to establish and reinforce to all human beings this lie; I am not lovable. Satan plants the lie in our minds, our broken self-embraces it as accurate and our society reinforces the lie at every juncture.

At home, children are openly shown more love if they behave correctly. In households with more than one child, favoritism is almost impossible not to practice. By elementary school, there is beginning to be groups of children who are "in" and those who are "out." It only grows worse by middle school. If you don't dress in the right clothes and have the right circle of friends the message sent is, *"You aren't lovable if you aren't pretty, athletic or smart."* As young adults, if you aren't married by around thirty the message is sent you are defective. If you do marry and end up getting divorced you receive the same reinforcement for the message you've had all your life. For those who stay married, too often life wears them down as the *"you aren't lovable"* message is thrown in their face regularly by their unhappy spouse.

Love is so conditional through all of life; we often find our lives being fueled by performance. If I get better grades, I will be more lovable. If I go to a more prestigious school; if I make a lot of money; if I have a measure of success, I will be more worthy of love. When I get that promotion, buy that home, or own that sports car, then I will be somebody. Many people volunteer at church or charities merely to make themselves feel better about their life. Every organization in existence is based on conditions and performance to belong. The entire world system reinforces to you and me that we are not lovable unless we are willing to dance to their drum beat.

I was thinking about church membership. Every church has their creed, their own set of pet beliefs, their quirks that are valued. The church says to us we want to extend the unconditional love of Jesus to you. Now if you will just jump through these five or ten hoops, you can be part of our group! Once you jump through all those hoops and become part, there will be a whole new set of regulations to keep if you want to keep your happy place in the group.

God forbid if you violate any of the things your particular association values. You will find out that even the church, an organization that is to represent Jesus Christ on planet earth is governed strictly by very conditional love as well.

It is interesting to me that God's one requirement for us is to be in his family is to believe the Gospel. He loves us the same whether we do or not. The moment we accept his forgiveness through

Christ, we are part of his forever family on earth. The adoption is forever. I cannot do anything to remove me from the family.

I was wondering what the local church would look like if it modeled the way Christ treats us. There would be no membership role. You are already a member if you are a Christian. Your baptism would be to show others you love the Lord and want to follow him, not as part of a membership requirement.

I've started to think the whole membership thing is so we can attempt to control you. We can put giving expectations on you and serving expectations to benefit our club, rather than teaching you to have a personal relationship with Jesus and let him be the motivation for what you do in your life.

If you sense some anger from me here, you would be correct. I committed adultery as a pastor in 2000. I was not caught. I admitted to being too close to someone emotionally, and that was enough to set many wheels in motion. I was sent off to a rehab place to help put me back together again. While I was there, I got a deep sense that I was to return to our church to prepare it to continue without me. I was not going to be allowed to stay there indefinitely, but it wasn't ready to survive without me.

I went back from the treatment, humbled and went about the task of preparing a growing ministry to continue growing without the leader they had known since 1992. I carried out the mission. In 2004, I confessed the full story to our staff and then to our elders. I remember being questioned about my ability to lead if they decided to keep me. I said, "*I have been leading these last three years since the failure. I have overhauled the ministry. I have led a campaign to build a new worship center, and it is nearly ready to move into. I am the same as I was during those three years. The only difference is your perception of me. The issue isn't whether I can lead; it is whether you can follow!*"

In a private meeting with our elders, I told them this process would reveal what they believed about the gospel, about leadership, and about forgiveness. I was asked to resign. Part of me agreed with the decision. What happened next, was not acceptable to me. I believe leadership and being loved as a brother should be two separate issues.

Where do you go when your world is crumbling around you? Where do you go when all your friends and social network for the last twelve years are at one place? Gayle and I wanted to go and worship at our church. We planned to slide in late, slip out early and cause no disruption. We wanted to be at our church with our friends. We went to worship and sat in the back. Many people hugged us and told us they were praying. It felt terrific to be able to be there.

The next week I got a call from one of the elders. He said, "*Some of the people were uncomfortable with you being at church and we are going to ask you not to come back for a period yet to be determined.*" The thing that irritated me the most about this is it was contrary to what I taught for twelve years. Our church was built on loving people however they came through the doors. One of our core values was to accept people broken and battered by life and love them back to life.

There was something wrong to tell someone who had already repented and confessed all his sin not to come to worship. What I came to see during this time was "The church people," and the "The church organization" are two different animals. I've come to love "The church people," while pretty much despising "The church organization." The organization may as well have echoed Satan's lie, "*If you are a good boy, then we will love you.*" Even the church organization reinforces the enemies lie, "*You are not lovable the way you are.*"

Six years after I was asked to no longer attend, I read with interest, "*Why I Stayed: The Choices I Made in My Darkest Hour.*[11]" This is Gayle Haggard's story. Her husband Ted Haggard had planted and pastored a church in Colorado Springs, Colorado. I will not retell their story here that is not my purpose. As I read the book, I found my anger boiling over to the point I wanted to throw the book against the wall. I found myself cursing some of the decisions that were made by people in leadership over the Haggards. The clear message sent to men who have given their lives to serve the people is, *"We love you as long as you are serving us, but if you let us down you are no longer lovable or welcome."*

I have been a member of four different churches now that have had moral failures among pastors. I've endured two youth pastors' failures, two senior pastors' failure and one worship pastor's failure. I also personally know many other men who have endured the fallout of moral failures. I'm not sure many people realize how traumatic this is for both the minister and his family. If you work in a secular position and fail in this way it is tough on the family but does not affect your livelihood in most cases. In ministry, your failure becomes a public issue. Your entire family is humiliated. You also lose your ability to make a living. The church almost always removes you, and no other church will hire you.

The man has to attempt to salvage his marriage, find a way to make a living, often will be forced to relocate as well. The spouse and children are forced to go from having a husband and dad who was a pillar of the community to being gossiped about for months and years to come. Part of this is merely the consequences of sin, and I own that. Part of it is a public mockery of why Jesus Christ died for our sin by the group who is supposed to be offering the message of redemption to a broken world.

Pastors are men. Most wounded men, who have no real understanding of what I'm writing here. Most people preparing for ministry aren't required to go through intense psychological counseling or work on their issues before entering the ministry. I now believe this is a colossal failure of the educational system that prepares ministers.   The countryside is littered with the broken carcasses of pastors and their families who have experienced some failure and have been discarded by the church they loved and served. The message sent is the same as was sent to us in elementary school. We love you if. . .

So, all my life through family, churches, organizations, and people, in general, I've received the same untrue message, "*You are not lovable.*" The truth is all human beings on planet earth have received the same message. *Buried at the core then, was not any particular failure. It is the brutal lie that I have believed most my life, "I am not worthy of love."* As my journey into the furnace of the core continued, I discovered there are a couple more closely related lies buried deep within.

CHAPTER SIX
CORE LIE TWO
I AM NOT ACCEPTABLE

I remember the first time I felt like I wasn't acceptable to others. It came during the awkward time of development between adolescence and puberty. Previous to this time of life, all the neighborhood kids in our small community went to the same elementary school. Society wasn't nearly as mobile then as it is now.

I knew every family in every home on our street and most surrounding streets. Back in that day, we moved from elementary school to the Junior High School, which included grades seven through nine. This was my first exposure to peer pressure. I met two guys, Jerry and Mike, who ultimately became my best friends during this time of life. One of my first memories of them was playing some basketball at Mike's house. I had a foul mouth at this point. To be friends with these guys meant no swearing allowed. I am not sure where that value came from, but the penalty was a punch in the shoulder. I got pretty beat up that first day but soon learned to be accepted by these two meant to clean up the language. That was a small price to pay and a positive improvment.

I was one year ahead of these guys in school, but we were the same age. Emotionally, I felt more at home with their class than my own. These two were very popular in school. They were kind of "preppies." They taught me how to dress to be part of the club. I remember some of the girls in their class regularly had parties. Jerry told me the girls didn't want to invite me, but he said to them if I didn't get asked he and Mike wouldn't attend either.

So, I got invited but didn't feel wanted. Life can be ruthless during these years. I received many messages about my shortcomings, like why the "in girls" didn't want me at their parties, etc. I had already developed some social layers of protection at this age. Sports and competition where my strong point during this time and I had developed a very cocky swagger. My mouth was bigger than I was. In games, if I did something outstanding, I could brag with the best of them. If I had you in a place of defeat, I was merciless with taunting. It is funny, the things I did as a kid to attempt to gain approval undermined the chances of that happening. My best efforts to fit in never seemed to work. I began to believe inside, for some reason I was not acceptable.

Nothing ever really changed as I grew older. Maybe you can relate to the feeling *"You are outside looking in."* That is how I've felt for as long as I can remember. If I failed, I wasn't good enough to be accepted. If I succeeded, I was too good to be accepted. I didn't understand that all of us are battling with the same lies, the same demons.

Gayle and I moved to our first pastorate in rural North Carolina. We were excited to move in and become part of the community. The first few years we didn't travel home for holidays because we wanted to be with our new church family. We soon realized, though the church seemed proud of their new pastor, *"We weren't from around there."* Maybe our expectations were too high. As pastor and family, we were the center of church life but on the outside of any other social life.

Gayle had a lifelong dream to be a stay-at-home mom. I had promised her early in our marriage I would work hard to provide so she could be home to raise our children. In that first church, they believed the adage, *"You keep him humble Lord, and we'll keep him poor."* We made enough to make it. The church was tiny and didn't pay much, so I went to work part-time for one of our families who owned a dairy farm. Rather than reevaluate to see if the church could pay a fair wage, they criticized Gayle for not pursuing work outside the home. Again, the message was sent and believed; you aren't acceptable the way you are. At that point in my life, all the things I'm writing about now were buried in the abyss of my spirit, and I had no clue they were there. The message since the fall of man has been, *"You are not acceptable."* All our social institutions, family, schools, organizations and even churches reinforce that lie.

Over time, I succumbed to the message in the lie. I fully embraced it as true. I noticed while I was in an essential position people acted as if they valued me. When I no longer was in that position or community, it appeared no one cared anything about me.

I remember after we moved from Chesapeake, I took all the initiative to stay in contact with the people I valued. After some time, I realized, few of them were ever calling me to see how I was. Once in a great while, I'd get a random call from someone who wondered about me but not many. I experimented with this. I consciously refused to call most the people for a period to see if any would initiate a phone call to me. I can come up with many reasons why people didn't call. We are all busy! When I'm out of sight, I'm out of mind. But the message I heard was we don't need you anymore. You have nothing to offer us now, so you aren't acceptable to us. We wish you well but don't value you enough to want you as part of our lives.

After a while, I decided the same about them. We will act like good friends when we see each other, but neither of us has the time or energy to stay in touch. Such is the message of life. All of us are so consumed with our stuff; this is the message we send unwittingly to others. We are all disposable! I. am very grateful for the few friends who have stayed in touch over the years.

Being accepted is such a significant part of our lives. All of us want to feel like we are a valued member of something. The problem is all of us are like hogs at a feeding trough while trying to get our own needs met; we are oblivious to others around us doing the same. This desire is so strong; we are often willing to go through initiations, hazing, and whatever hurdle is required to have our name on a membership roll.

I remember seeing a group of men pictured in the newspaper. They all had funny hats on and white aprons. They were being initiated into a lodge. I remember thinking, what would possess a man to wear that outfit and then allow himself to be pictured in the newspaper. This intense need for acceptance is the fuel behind that decision. When you reach a certain point in life, you can see all the cultural trends are fueled by our massive need for acceptance. The powerful pull comes because at our core, we believe the lie. We feel we are not acceptable so we are desperate to prove ourselves to others so we can be accepted. The problem is whatever we do is never enough.

I think about the dynamic of this pattern in my own life. Looking solely from my perspective, I can see my strong need to be accepted manifested. I had become an integral part of our church in Williamsport, PA, as a volunteer. Anytime a lack was mentioned in that church I volunteered. Later, believing I was called to ministry, Gayle and I moved to Winston-Salem, NC.

Upon starting to attend another church, it felt like starting the acceptance thing all over again. The church had sixty college students who had been key people in their home churches. Now we were all like small fish in a big pond. It took a while, but while working 35 hours a week, and going to college carrying 12 credit hours, I taught Sunday School, sang in the choir, started a Saturday Morning outreach and led a youth Bible Study. I finally had achieved a similar status as I had in our home church. It nearly killed me, but I felt like I gained some measure of acceptance. That is until; I was offered the pastorate in my first church. That offer came during my last semester of college. When I told the pastor, I was thinking about taking the offer, everything changed.

As I filled the pulpit each Sunday at another church, as I was no longer useful at the college church, the message was embedded more deeply than ever. You are nothing more than a useful commodity; your entire value is what you bring to the table. When you are no longer contributing to our cause, you are no longer needed. Therefore, you are no longer acceptable to us. It was worse than not being accepted; it was as if I never existed.

Here I sit typing and thinking about my current status in life. I still feel the same desire to be accepted and valued at my work for the utility and at my church. With my eyes wide open, I look at what it costs and what the payback is on the investment. I know I am not willing to pay the price anymore. I see the message will ultimately be the same. *"Thanks for your service, sorry you are leaving, and have a good life!"* Having tried so hard for so long, I'm nearly ready to accept the lie is true. I'm not acceptable. As if not being lovable or acceptable was enough to overwhelm the best of us, I discovered one more core lie that will be the content of the next chapter.

CHAPTER SEVEN
CORE LIE THREE
I AM NOT ADEQUATE

I remember hearing Danny Sullivan interviewed on TV after winning the 1985 Indianapolis 500. The announcer asked the question, *"What motivates you?"* Danny's answer has always stuck with me, and it was over 30 years ago now. His answer was, *"The fear of failure."*

If we could cut open men and see what is buried deep within, this fear of failure would be in most. Many of us would say the fear of failure is a driving force in our lives. The fear of not measuring up, not being good enough, or letting people down will either drive you to succeed at any cost or paralyze you from even trying. But in either case, it is because at our core we have believed the lie that we don't have what it takes.

The drive to succeed then is an attempt to build a social layer of protection. It will produce a public image of success for others to see while down deep we are not convinced. There are few more obvious illustrations of this than Tiger Woods. I'm a huge Tiger fan, so I'm not beating him up. Tiger built this perfect image of success. He was every advertiser's dream. His endorsement deals were staggering. Tiger had both social and secret layers of protection.

When Tiger's secret layer became public the social layer dissolved before the entire world's eyes.

Often even in success, a man will feel like he is a fraud and the achievement will vanish as quickly as it came. For the person who believes the lie and isn't willing to try, it is easier not to try than to try and reinforce the lie is true.

Every little boy has this fear of failure in him. It is the fear to try new things. It is the fear to stand in front of classmates and be questioned by a teacher. It is the fear of trying out for a sports team. It is the fear of going for the first day of a new job. Many of those concerns could be alleviated by an involved, active, nurturing dad. The lack of committed fathers in our society is partially why this sense of inadequacy is so prevalent among men. But it is deeper than that!

My first recollection of being sent the message of inadequacy was as a nine-year-old trying out for Little League Baseball. ® Back in those days, people were cut. Each team could have fifteen players, and not everyone made the team. In fact, not everyone was even picked to try out for a team! If you didn't make the team, you had to play morning league with eight-year-olds and tryout again the following year. I remember hearing my name called as being cut the final night of tryouts on a cold, Pennsylvania, spring evening. Most of my friends had made the team they had tried out for, and it reinforced the lie I already believed, *"You just aren't good enough."*

I recall the first time I was reluctant to try something for fear of failure as well. I was about ten years old and was taking swimming lessons at the YMCA. It was wintertime; the pool area wasn't very warm. I didn't like going there very much. It was right after school, and by the time we got done, it was dark outside. I remember standing by the pool freezing and wishing I could just go home. The instructor ordered us all to jump in the pool, and I just stood there.

I can still hear, "*Ranck, shape up or ship out!*" I wanted to run out the door and go home, but I reluctantly jumped in the pool.

Another example that comes to mind is from high school. Our school had a gymnastics team. We were the only school in the area at the time that did. We traveled to other schools and did gym shows that were a big hit. When I was young, my cousin had a trampoline in his backyard. He went into the military and gave it to me. So, from the time I was about twelve years old, I had been jumping on the trampoline in the privacy of my backyard. With no one watching, I could risk learning new things. I became quite good on the trampoline.

By the time I got to high school, the gymnastics coach had heard about me. Everyone loved watching a trampolinist in the show; it was one of the highlights. I remember as a sophomore my first year on the team, getting up to perform in front of a packed gymnasium. A big spotlight shone on me as the announcer broadcast, "*Next up on the trampoline, the ringmaster himself, Scott Ranck!*" It was a proud moment, and I did not have that fear or sense of inadequacy. I knew I was good and I could do it.

For all three years of high school, I would go to gymnastics practice and show off on the trampoline. The coach would come to me regularly and say, "*Scottie, why don't you work on the rings and parallel bars and learn something new.*" I never ventured off the safety of the trampoline. My thought was, "*Are you crazy, why would I go over there and be a rookie when I can stay here and be the star?*" My performance on the trampoline gave me an image of success; I wasn't willing to risk revealing my inadequacy by doing something in which I thought I would not excel.

As I got older, I remember having that deep sense of, "*I don't think I have what it takes to do this thing.*" I have sensed that at the start of every new venture. I remember at twenty-five years of age preparing to go back to college. I had the school's literature with the course descriptions I was taking. *"I don't know that I can do this,"* was the thought in my mind. All through college, I would over prepare for tests, take them, feel like I didn't do well, and then receive my grade, and it would be an A. I graduated from college first in my class, *Summa Cum Laude*, but still had this under riding lack of belief in my ability to accomplish life's challenges.

One last personal observation is stemming from this concept of believing the lie; I'm not adequate. Over the years, I've had the opportunity to be on leadership teams where I wasn't the senior leader. I have a sharp mind, quick wit and a good sense of things when I'm in the support role. Often the best decisions are crystal clear to me. However, when I am the senior leader of the team, I am regularly frozen by indecision. Everything seems cloudier to me. I've come to see, that is from believing this lie. In the former instance the final decision will be a reflection on someone else; in the latter, the reflection is on me!

As we put these three cores lies together, something very sinister appears. If I am not loveable, acceptable or adequate unless I perform to some illusionary standard, too much is riding on everything. **Too much is riding on everything!** All my activity becomes an opportunity for accolade or indictment of me as a person. Every decision will either bolster my social image or reveal the lies are true. Every opportunity becomes a chance for pride or despair. With each attempt I make to be a good husband, my whole self is on the line waiting for the reaction from Gayle. With her smile, I passed the test, with a frown I'm a loser.

All of life becomes a big test and every employer, every significant person in our world has the power to declare me lovable, acceptable, and adequate or not. My personal view of myself rises and falls with every outside decree. This is a vicious way to live. Dr. Jim Dobson said this is how all of us form our view of self. Our view of ourselves is built on how we think others perceive us.

All these things I've written about so far contain a common element. No one and I mean no one can get through life without getting hurt. We are wounded by believing these lies. We are hurt by people, our own choices and life circumstances. No one gives us much clear teaching on dealing with hurt in a healthy way. I'm going to pause in the journey, and the next chapter is going to deal with handling hurt.

CHAPTER EIGHT
THE "HURT FAMILY TREE"

On my journey to the core, I had a growing irritability. It took the form of discontentment with nearly everything in my life. I found myself "armchair pastoring" our church. I was negative, critical and nitpicking most everything. I rarely left a church service inspired or uplifted on the contrary I'd leave irritated and fuming about something. I could go to a secular meeting at a builder association or the like and leave feeling like they didn't know what they were doing. I could be negative about Gayle or our family or where I lived or where I worked. The negativity seemed to splash acid on people around me. I had a growing awareness this wasn't good. I invited the men at our men's ministry to help me figure myself out. I permitted them to tell me the truth no matter how brutal it would be to hear. What I heard that night was, *"Whatever the problem is, it isn't our church, your job or your family. And if you don't figure it out, your ministry will be very limited!"*

The next morning in my time with the Lord, I pleaded with him to reveal to me what was wrong. I was reading in the Psalms and came to Psalm 73 that morning. Psalm 73 is a believer who when seeing wicked people prosper, he almost lost his faith. I came to verse 21, *"Then I realized my heart was bitter, and I was all torn up inside.*" As only he can do, the Spirit of God quietly spoke to me and said, *"There is your problem, you are bitter, and bitterness is a sin."* I slipped off my chair and got on my knees and confessed to the Lord I was bitter and asked him to forgive me. This is the only time in my 40 plus years of being a Christian; I felt a huge load lift from me. As that morning passed, it was like the fog in my mind began to clear. Over the course of the week, the Lord unpacked for me the "Hurt Family Tree." Bitterness is the fruit of not dealing with hurt biblically. Here is what I've learned.

When we are hurt, it is as if someone plants a seed in us that is full of possibility. At that point, I have many options. I may choose to seek revenge. I may decide to medicate it, or I may decide to rehearse it by "telling myself stories." When I do this, I add my commentary to the injury in my head and embellish the story with my perceptions of what happened. It is pure fiction. I may also then rehash the story with others, complete with my fabrications. When I do that the seed of hurt sown in my life is watered, fertilized and cultivated. It grows. Hurt will quickly bloom into anger. For men, especially the shift from hurt to anger can be so quick, we don't realize we are hurt. We just think we are angry. Show me an angry man, and I'll show you an injured man who hasn't handled it well. My last choice when hurt is present is I can choose to forgive the offender.

I want to spend some time on option three and what happens when I nurture the seedling of hurt. My hurt turns to anger. Anger should be a red flag in most cases to examine where I've been hurt. The Bible says in Ephesians 4:26-27, *"And don't sin by letting anger control you. Don't let the sun go down while you are still angry.* ***For anger gives a foothold to the devil.***"

When I am angry because of a hurt, and I don't deal with it quickly, that anger will grow into resentment. Resentment is hurt taking deeper root into my soul. Resentment is focused toward the one who hurt me, but it is stronger than just hurt. When I allow resentment to stay and I still have not forgiven, resentment will grow a root of bitterness.

Bitterness is a wild root. It will grow rapidly and randomly through your entire garden and bring forth fruit everywhere. It will spring up at your job, in your family at your church or basically wherever you are. Bitterness is the devil's foothold that comes from not dealing with hurt and anger the way God prescribed. I cannot be resentful or bitter unless I have mishandled a hurt. That is why that morning reading Psalm 73; I sensed God tell me being bitter was my sin. It didn't matter who did what to me, it was only because I didn't choose to forgive way back the little seed of hurt grew into an entire garden (life) overrun with a wild root and weeds that choked the life out of me. It became clear to me when the root of bitterness is growing in my life; it chokes out the fruit of the spirit. [12]

This hurt family tree, then looks like this. Someone does something to hurt me. Hurt gives birth to anger; anger's offspring is resentment and resentment give birth to the bitterness that poisons all of life. This family tree needs to come to extinction! When I confessed the sin of being bitter, it was like cutting the weed bushes back and pulling up the roots.

With bitterness gone, I now have to backtrack starting with the resentment directed at the person or situation that hurt me originally. The cure to resolve that resentment is twofold. I need to confess my sin of allowing that resentment to form by mishandling the original hurt and secondly, I need to forgive the one who hurt me. When that happens the root of bitterness is uprooted, the plants of resentment are removed and ultimately the seed of hurt that was sown in my life dies. The hurt family tree can all die off. Then regular maintenance will be required to keep my life free of bitterness.

The bottom line is when I choose anything other than forgiving, just as God for Christ sake has forgiven me,[13] I set this progression in motion, and ultimately **my reaction to the hurt, will hurt me far worse** than the original hurt itself. I'm not minimizing how badly we can be hurt either.

Any counselor will tell you, the stories we tell ourselves about our hurt, cause more significant damage than the wrong done to us. Let me illustrate with an extreme injury. Let's say a young girl is sexually abused by someone. That abuse is wrong and incredibly hurtful. It is monumentally difficult for an abuse victim even to consider forgiving the offender. But through my experience counseling people in this situation, the most considerable damage comes from how the person interprets the abuse. When they believe they were partially at fault, or they tell themselves I am now somehow "dirty or marred" as a person and don't deserve to be loved. Or other such untrue stories common among abuse victims. The abuse was terrible but, the aftermath of self-loathing and deceptions cause more severe damage.

I've come to see believing the three lies described above; I'm not loveable, acceptable or adequate can produce enough hurt to grow bitterness. Then pile on all the events and people that inflict hurt through our lives, and you can understand why so many are bitter.

The unraveling of bitterness, resentments, anger, and hurt may be a lengthy process. I would say it depends on a few issues. First, more significant abuses take more work than lesser blows. Second, how long the bitterness has been present may affect the recovery. How much the hurt has been nurtured and how deeply it is rooted in the person's life may impact healing. Finally, the person's ability to trust God may make healing come more quickly. The unraveling of the hurt family tree could take a moment, a week, a decade or a lifetime.

So, I got on my knees and confessed my bitterness. I admitted my resentments. I forgave offenders, and I asked those I hurt in bitterness to forgive me. Gayle tells me I'm more at peace; she can see it and feel it. To me, one of the most amazing things happened. I cannot remember ever sleeping all night. I blamed it on a small bladder! I always was up at least once during the night and often a couple of times. In the weeks since this discovery, I have regularly slept from the time I hit the bed till the alarm goes off in the morning without waking at all during the night. I find that amazing! This part of the journey has been so helpful for me and many I've been able to share it with, and I hope it helps you too.

In the next section, we will continue the journey. The great thing about a lie is it is not true! This journey to the core is difficult and painful and wouldn't be worth doing except for the very last thing I found buried underneath all the layers and all the lies. You see, I've known for some time there was something wrong. I wasn't finding answers in the pat solutions offered at church or anywhere else. This search is much like after a move when your garage is packed full of boxes. You know there is something you need in one of the boxes, and you need to find it. You are willing to dig and dig because you know there is a prize waiting for you in there somewhere. Much like that, after wading through all the stuff, I've written about so far, at the center of it all I found...

PART TWO
REDEEMING THE CORE

CHAPTER NINE
BURIED TREASURE

As I began this journey, I had no idea where it would all end. I did think I would uncover some significant hurt from my early life that scarred me. I found many things on the journey to the core that was hurtful. It was interesting to me the emotion I felt as I wrote the first part of this book. Initially, I thought the core was a dark place. What I discovered when I cleared all the other junk out of the way was a wonderful thing. I will unfold all those discoveries in part two.

The first discovery was an exceptional find. It was based on the truth of several passages of Scripture that have taken on a fresh meaning to me. I found a person created in the image of God![14] This concept has never been the first thought I've had about myself or for that matter anyone else. But that truth changes the way I think about me and the way I feel about others.

I've been open about my negative thoughts toward the guy on the street corner holding the cardboard sign asking for money. Everything changes when I look at that guy through the lens of this book. I saw layers and layers of hurt, pain, shame, resentments, bitterness, and fear but buried under all of it is a person created in the image of God. It gives me a greater sense of empathy for him.

How much abuse and pain does it take to bury a person with so much negativity you can scarcely see any flicker of light in them? Every person you will ever meet on this planet has been created in God's image. But far too often that image isn't evident.

What exactly does it mean to be created in the image of God? Theologians put forth several ideas what they believe that to mean. Many will say it means humans have intellect, emotion, and will. Some will add we have a built-in moral compass because God is moral. Some argue backward from human to divine and say we are alive, moral; thinking beings, therefore, our creator must have the same traits. I would say it is more than all those things.

Since Jesus is both perfect man and deity, I believe we can see what it means to be created in God's image by looking at the human side of Jesus. His humanity is the picture of what God intended for all of us before sin entered the world. The Scriptures teach that Jesus was the exact duplicate of the Father, so much so that Jesus said, "*If you have seen me, you've seen the Father.*"[15] Any likeness to God in human beings is buried so deeply under all our sin, shame and woundedness that it can only be discovered through redemption. I don't believe any self-discovery or self-help is adequate. There needs to be a true remedy for all the issues discussed in part one.

A few years ago, on a trip to my mom's home in South Williamsport, PA., my sister, Michelle, brother, Eric and my wife, Gayle and I were rummaging around in mom's attic. We found some old autographed pictures of people who went on to be stars. Ella Fitzgerald and Ozzie Nelson were two of the most prominent stars we had. Instantly, we all thought we found something of great value. At this time, I've not heard if they have any value or not. The point is this, they have value, and it is whatever someone is willing to pay for them. To say they are worth a thousand dollars doesn't mean anything unless someone will pay a thousand dollars to own them.

God values you and me as human beings created in his image so much that he was willing to send his son to this earth to redeem us. Redeem means to repurchase something, to pay the price for ransom. Again, scholars quibble over to whom God would have to make payment. The simple answer is, to be true to his nature payment had to be made for our violations of his law. God is both just and merciful and to be faithful to both those innate qualities an innocent party had to meet the judicial requirements of the law. When a governor or president in our country issues a pardon to a guilty convict real justice is not served. Mercy is shown but not justice. Humans cannot be both just and merciful at the same time in the strictest sense. We can be one or the other but not both. Justice means the full penalty for a wrong is exacted. Mercy implies judgment is withheld from someone who rightfully deserves punishment. So, for a judge to give the total sentence justice demands says he cannot show mercy at the same time.

I believe Jesus by dying on the cross and resurrecting from the grave is the answer. In Jesus death, the full payment of all sin was paid, meaning God's justice was fully satisfied. Because God's justice was satisfied, he can now satisfy his mercy by allowing us to go free when we embrace the Savior.[16] The problem is we've made the gospel so simple and shallow in our presentation and understanding its power is not unleashed. Modern Christianity has many constituents who are living from one or all of the layers we've discussed. The power of the gospel has never penetrated to the core; therefore, there is neither freedom nor joy. Joy is a valid indicator a person has an acute awareness of how severely the image of God has been marred by them and what a miraculous thing it is that they have been redeemed.

So, I discovered that in the forgiving and healing power of the gospel, God begins to bring out his image in you and me so others will be able to see glimpses of the divine in us. It is fascinating to see how attractive God's attributes are to people. When you study the life of Jesus in the New Testament, you see people being drawn to him who were repulsed by the religious crowd.

Nothing has changed much in two thousand years! Jesus says things like, *"God didn't send his Son into the world to condemn it, but to save it."*[17] His life was true to that, and people felt loved, valued and included when they were in his presence, no matter who they were or what they had done. That will be further evidence the gospel has reached to your deepest parts. People who may not darken the door of a church will find you approachable and often will be drawn to you.

In no way do I feel I've arrived nor have this mastered. But I have seen some glimpses of what I'm writing here. I will share one experience I had recently. I was on a flight from Tampa to Charlotte for work. I was flying Southwest Airlines because of the direct flight; low price and they are my favorite. Southwest has open seating. The flight was full. I had an aisle seat about three-quarters of the way back. There was another gentleman in the window seat. I was praying the Lord would put someone in the seat that would be open to hearing about him. Eventually, a young lady asked if she could sit there. Later in our conversation during the flight, the young lady told me the reason she sat in that seat was as she was coming down the aisle from the front of the plane all she could see was my face. Her exact words were, *"You looked like someone who was full of joy, and I wanted to find out about that."*

All I can say is I must have been having a good day. We talked the entire flight and prayed together at the conclusion. She thanked me for all the things I shared with her and said she felt so much better. When we parted, she said, *"Thank you, Pastor Scott,"* and hugged me. I must say, based on the things she told me, I felt very much like Jesus and some of his encounters with women in the Bible. Her life was full of shame, but she was attracted to Jesus in me.

That kind of ministry doesn't happen when you are living from the religious protective layer. I want to clarify that statement. You may have encounters where you peddle your message when living from the religious layer. You may even have encounters where you will talk someone into praying a "sinner's prayer." I hate to say this, but it won't be life changing. You will not have encounters where people are attracted to you and ask you about the hope that is in you.[18] You will not have meetings that are core to core thus life transforming. I have had far too many of those superficial type encounters.

What I discovered at my core is a man who was created in the image of God. But there is more. Psalm 139:13-18 is a fantastic passage. These verses teach that God was active weaving us together as an elegant tapestry while yet in our mother's womb. All the pieces come together when joined with other texts that teach God has a plan for our lives, and he gifts us with what we need to accomplish that plan.[19] The enemy's strategy all along has been to blind us through the maze of pain and layers. He keeps us trapped by our shame, hurts, and bitterness, so we never experience the fullness of our redemption.

So deep within me under all the protective layers I had established, beneath all the lies I believed my entire life; beneath the bitterness from unresolved hurt was this buried treasure and experiences of truth from the Father to counter all the lies. The remainder of this second section of the book is going to delve into some personal encounters I've had with the Lord and what he is teaching me to counter all the enemy's attacks.

CHAPTER TEN
I AM LOVED

started this journey to the core before my public failure in 2000. I knew something wasn't right with me. My good friend Willie P. introduced me to the concepts of recovery used in the AA and NA[20] meetings. I had purchased a workbook[21] and worked the twelve steps. This was my first introduction to doing any real introspection.

That study uncovered so much that instinctively I believed every human would benefit from a similar exercise. As I became more honest, open and willing more things became apparent to me that needed attention. I began to peel away the layers. The things I learned in my formal study of the Bible and things I learned in recovery helped me with some discoveries along the way.

But because I believed the lie that was woven into the fabric of my being that I was not lovable, hearing how much God loved me never registered. I listened to that message often but never was able to replace the lie with the truth. I have an observation. There could be a correlation between the inability to believe God loves me unconditionally and the quality of love experienced from other people. It seems extremely difficult to grasp a concept that is entirely foreign to our experience.

I had all the garbage I've waded through in this book stirring under the surface of my life. What started as a very wholesome, supportive working relationship with a female in my workplace started deteriorating. A harmonious personality blend, some physical attraction, some level of neediness and large blocks of time together became the formula for disaster. I violated my marriage vows. I went against everything I believed and taught. I broke major friendships. Worst of all I wasn't caught, so I lived with that additional crushing weight of cognitive dissonance[22] for a couple of months. This whole saga completely drained the life from me spiritually and emotionally till I was spent. There was nothing left but a shell.

Let me hit the pause button for a minute to review what we have learned so far. It is incredible to realize this big mess I created for myself was a huge problem. But it wasn't my core problem. All this confusion was merely a symptom. It was the unraveling of life not lived from a healthy core! Often it takes this type of crisis for someone to be motivated to do this kind of hard work on themselves. We could ask the question when someone's junk comes to light. *"Is it good or is it bad?"* As hurtful as these unveilings can be, often they become the stimulus to find help and healing. As long as we can maintain our charade without having our true selves exposed, we will play the game.

Now let's get back to the story. I had admitted to Gayle and our church leaders I was emotionally attached to someone that wasn't my wife. That was my social protective layer. The elders called a meeting where they grilled me for information which I didn't give. They decided to send me to Perdido Key, Florida for two weeks to enter a counseling center for broken pastors. This story was in my first book but was not written in a way that the full impact could be felt.

When I got on the plane to fly to Florida, I had a tiny bit of relief because some people knew part of my story. But the weight of the full truth was heavy on me. I knew I was in big trouble. My emotional battering began years before this. All that I've written about the nature of life, plus ministry setbacks, losing my staff dream team, and having families leave our church angry over what

I considered progress all contributed. My inability to handle life on life's terms paired with all those painful things made me a prime candidate to do something stupid.

Then the months of verbal unfaithfulness followed by physical unfaithfulness killed me. I had no resources left to deal with the full truth. Adultery often brings divorce; I was sure that would be my fate. Infidelity, when committed by pastors, brings instant firing and public humiliation along with untold damage to the church ministry and families that I cared for deeply. It is hard for people to grasp when you do something like this, how compartmentalized it is.

I genuinely still felt love for my wife and our church. I didn't want to destroy anything. I wasn't some evil, skirt-chasing, church wrecking criminal. The religious, social and secret layers I had painstakingly constructed were coming unglued. I had a flight and two weeks away to figure this mess out, but I was exhausted. I was like a terrified little boy that was in deep trouble but I had no one I trusted who could help me.

Since I was going to Pensacola, Florida the flight landed in Alabama. The counselor and his wife picked me up. I was whipped, it was a Sunday afternoon. We had about an hour ride to get to the counseling center and my apartment, where I hoped to get some rest.

They had to run a few errands, and I had no option but to go with them. It seemed to take forever. We finally arrived at the center, and I was given the tour. Then I moved into my little apartment where I would spend the next two weeks alone. If you know anything about the massive amounts of emotional pain I was dealing with at this time, the last thing I wanted is to be alone and quiet.

Activity and noise are great friends to those who are fighting demons. I had a couple of hours of daylight left, and my only wheels were a bicycle but I road till after dark. I was part way across Alabama before I turned around and came back. The two big positive things about this time were 1) I was at the beach in January and 2) I had no responsibility.

I started the three hours a day counseling sessions Monday. I went from 10:00 a.m. to 1:00 p.m. each day. I had about an hour of homework to do that I perceived more like busy work. I had three days under my belt that wasn't doing anything for me. I got up each morning and went for a run on the beach before the counseling session. I would go back to my apartment and clean up and eat then head to the counselor. Once I was out of counseling, I was on my own with basically nothing to do and no way to go anywhere. I would take long walks on the beach or around the key. I was alone with my thoughts, and the weight of my failure that I thought was going to ultimately kill me. I felt depressed. I was at the lowest point I have ever known in my entire life. I felt like if something didn't happen during my time at the counseling center, I would not go back home. I had no clear plan; I just was going to go somewhere farther south in Florida and run from the disaster looming in Virginia. I wondered why God didn't just kill me and put me out of my misery.

So, Thursday morning I get up and head over to the beach to run. I recall it was quite chilly that morning. As I was running, the beach was entirely deserted. I was about ten minutes into a forty-minute run when a powerful impression came into my mind. The voice said, "*I love you son!*" Instinctively I knew God was talking to me.

That simple statement cut me to the core, and I wept like a baby for nearly thirty minutes. The impression was so clear, strong and unexpected the result was I believed and experienced God loved me. I was in wonder and awe. I could have understood if he had told me he was disappointed. Or if he said, "*You dropped the ball this time son.*"

Sometimes now, eighteen years later, I find it hard to believe at the lowest point of my life is when he decided to allow me to experience his unconditional love. There is probably no better time to convince someone you love them unconditionally than when they can point to no logical reason for that love.

I remember having an overwhelming desire to be in his presence following that encounter. All I could think about was reading the Gospels in the New Testament. I read the bulk of Matthew's Gospel in one sitting. It seemed I was reading with new eyes. The Lord's presence was so tangible in my life during this time. He made it clear to me I would have to return home and repair my marriage and develop the church not to need me because he would not allow me to stay long term. I was also acutely aware for the first time in my life that all would be well because I was loved with a never-ending, unconditional love.

There is a difference between love and the next core truth I came to experience. They are so related the traits are often said together, love and accept. Acceptance is different and comes out of that deep love. The next chapter will delve into replacing the lie that I am not acceptable with the truth.

CHAPTER ELEVEN
I AM ACCEPTED

Fast forward nine years from the scenario you just read about, the encounter on the beach run. I had remained at the church three and a half years past that experience. Then Gayle and I moved to Florida. The struggle of trying to figure out who I am apart from my ministry role was tough. We were now strangers in a new town. No one knew anything about my background.

I often envied people who lived in the same town all their lives and they could rehearse everyone's history. They seemed like they belonged. They fit; everywhere they went people knew them and their families. That wasn't the case for us. Our family began moving in 1979 when we left our home and family in Pennsylvania. Every move brought a fresh sense of not belonging. *"You must not be from around here,"* was heard too many times. The feeling of being on the outside looking in was something I began to realize had been with me most my life.

In my role with a natural gas utility, I had the opportunity to travel some. On those trips away, I would sense a profound loneliness. I felt like I was alone in the world. Like I didn't belong where I was, but there was no way to peel back thirty years and go home again either. One day the Lord decided to address this and here is the account of Him letting me know I had believed a lie.

I was at a beautiful, tropical resort for a work conference. People dream about coming to this place. Many save money for a year or more to visit this location on a vacation they wished would never end. This particular night, I was sitting outside watching the palm branches in the gentle breeze. The moon was nearly full and lit the sky, reflecting off the exotic tropical swimming pool. If the picture could have been captured on film, it could easily be used to lure the next group of paradise seekers to this place.

I was here alone, but not just alone, lonely. Loneliness is hard to describe but I've learned can be experienced even when with others. When I experience this kind of loneliness, it is a feeling that goes deep to the core of my being. It is the sense that no one else on this planet or beyond can know me and love me at the deepest places of my soul. I recall having this feeling as far back as childhood. I remember attempting to soothe it as a middle schooler by retreating to my sister's bedroom and listening to music. Particular times of the day seemed to be worse than others; early evening has been the worst time for me. Working late or working away from home, eating dinner or going for a walk alone allowed me to experience again that profound core loneliness that has been my lifetime companion.

Even as a Christian of many years, my relationship with God didn't slake this thirst for connection. This core loneliness has been my most prevalent and long-lasting pain, though for many, many years I didn't realize it. Dramatically, as only He could do, He revealed to me what I have needed to see all these years. Through years of soul searching, He chose to pull the curtains back and show me another buried treasure.

I headed out on my five-mile run, and I could tell from previous encounters, I was going to have a divine appointment. The movie reel started in my mind. These things for me are almost like I'm watching a show on the screen of my mind, but I have no clue where it is going or how it will end. That is why I believe they are divine communications. They always are true to Scripture and for me, have brought life change. This day's lesson would prove to be one of the most significant of my life. I believe the experience went all the way to the core of my psyche and gave me another long sought-after answer to the hunger of my soul.

It began with my son and my father. Lately, I've been noticing since my son is a married man and has his own home and yard, how much he is like my father. Both men were wired differently than me. Dad and Bub were tight for the few years they both were alive together. Both are somewhat quiet men. Both wise beyond their years, both listen more than talk; both men love to grow things, tinker with things and both are pretty content to be home. Dad would have developed the whole backyard into a garden if mom would have let him and Bub is the same! Both men enjoy inventing things and are curious about many areas of life. Both always had some side business going.

With that connection between the two firmly in my head, the scene continued. Dad as a very young man was in the Army Air Corp. As only a twenty-year-old he finds himself far from home in the European Theater during WWII. Dad was a nose gunner on a B-24 Bomber. Their mission was to fly from Italy several hours one way, bomb the oil fields of Ploesti, Romania and hopefully return. Seeing dad in that situation through the eyes of a father instead of a son, thinking about Bub in the same situation, knowing his gentle nature and spirit, touched me deeply.

On mission number 17, dad's plane was shot down; his crew all bailed out, and they all were captured immediately upon hitting the ground. They were interned as POWs for several months. I thought about what it must have been like at dinner time and bedtime, thousands of miles from home, held by enemies and wondering if he would ever see his mom, dad or home again. Dad lost sixty pounds in a few short months. Ultimately, he was released and got to make it home. But the layers of pain from his life experience and additional pain added later was something I don't think he had the resources to unravel. In those days, you just sucked up your stuff and pressed on. Dad loved me the best he could but what he had to offer me emotionally wasn't enough.

The scene shifted to my mom. Mom was third youngest of eight children. Mom's oldest brother was killed by a street car when he was twelve years old. My grandfather was a drinker and womanizer and abusive towards my grandmother. Mom has told me stories of how as kids their dad would come home drunk and hit their mom, and the kids would circle their mom in an attempt to protect her. I got this mental picture of seven little puppies around one tiny bowl of food; they all were pushing and fighting, grubbing to get a little morsel. That picture accurately describes what it was like for those kids emotionally trying to get any attention from their mom. Attention from their dad was shaky at best.

So, how does someone grow up in that environment learning to fight for every little bit of attention you can get. Do you think in some way a person instantly changes when becoming a parent? Do you think they would have the resources all of a sudden to nurture their needy children? How does that happen when your emotional reservoir is empty? My mother loved me the best she could with what she had, but it wasn't enough.

I grew up with many unmet emotional needs, as does every human on the planet, but I still had a chance, maybe a future spouse would be able to meet all those needs and make me happy and fulfilled! What a massive expectation, doomed to failure that is placed on the shoulders of a spouse. Whomever you partner with will have some story of unmet childhood emotional needs as well. You can never take two imperfect, unhealthy people and put them together and magically have a healthy marriage! No wonder, so few marriages survive. So, though I have had the same incredible wife since 1973, who loves me devotedly, she isn't enough.

Solomon said in Ecclesiastes 3:11, "God *has made everything beautiful in its time and has **PLANTED ETERNITY IN THE HUMAN HEART**.*" Through these scenes, the Lord showed me no human being could meet an eternal need; their reservoir is too limited. No parents, no matter how balanced or healthy is enough, needs still go unmet. No spouse will ever be enough. It takes something of eternal, limitless reserve to meet the eternal need placed in our hearts.

Ephesians 1:5 New Living Translation says, "*God decided in advance to adopt us into his own family by bringing us to himself through Jesus Christ. This is what he wanted to do, and it gave him great pleasure.*" Adoption takes great effort, is driven by love and by choice. Being born into a family could mean any number of things. You may have been planned for and anticipated. You may have been a mistake and a nuisance! But adoption means someone is making an informed choice to want you, and legally make you part of their family. God does that for each of us who want to be included. He says, "*Yes, I've always wanted you, already made legal provisions to have you and I want to share my forever home with you. My emotional reservoir has no limits; I love you with an everlasting love! You are on the inside, connected, accepted, and loved never to be outside looking in again. You are forever and always related to me as my child, and you will never be alone again even if physically you are alone. Any joy you get from earthly relationships will be icing on the cake, but none of those relationships could ever be enough on its own!* All my life I've wanted to be known and still accepted, I've wanted to belong somewhere. Adoption into the divine family is my answer.

I am accepted and wanted by God for his forever family. Though this has been true in my life since I became a Christian, for many of the years I've not experienced the truth and fullness of these promises. This truth of my adoption counters the lie I am not acceptable.

As powerful as these two truths are; I am loved, and I am accepted, the third lie I believed is possibly the most difficult for a man. Believing the lie, "*I am not adequate, I'm not good enough,*" for a man cuts right into our strength. Many men fear failure more than anything else because it merely validates their wrong belief, they don't have what it takes. The Lord is teaching me; I have been looking for the remedy to this lie in all the wrong places.

CHAPTER TWELVE
I AM ADEQUATE
ad·e·quate adjective sufficient for a specific requirement[23]

The first exposure I had to see someone more than adequate but far less than perfect was the Sunday Willie Pegram stood in front of Believers Baptist Church and told his story. In the early days of my church experience, the people on the platform all looked and talked like they had their stuff together. It sent a message that maybe one day you may grow to this level of spiritual vigor and maturity, but it will take years! Most sermons I hear in church are telling me what a passage in the Bible said, but I have never heard much about the transformation process to get there. The pastor's message too often goes from his head to my head, and neither of our hearts is moved in the process.

Early in my pastorate at Believers, all I had done was preach the Bible and never let them see me sweat. I was approached by Willie P about the possibility of starting something within the church to help the sick and suffering addicts in our community. Willie is a recovering addict and had spoken all over the state and in various meetings, but he wondered why the church wasn't doing anything to help. We talked it over and became convinced the Lord wanted us to start something. This was in 1992, long before Celebrate Recovery[24] became a standard program in churches. I presented the idea to our deacons, the men who called the shots in our church. Remember this was a Baptist Church! The men said they weren't sure about the program, but they trusted me, so I got the green light to proceed.

Willie and I decided our strategy would be to let him tell his story in a Sunday Morning Worship Service and then invite people to join Willie the following week in a classroom setting.

The deacons said to me, "*You think at this church anyone will go in that classroom admitting they have a problem with drugs or alcohol?*" I responded, "*I don't know. All I know is I am supposed to allow this group to start.*"

The Sunday came, and Willie and I were in my office before the service. Willie asked me, "*Can I tell them the story about when I crapped my pants in front of the rescue mission?*" I said, "*Tell them anything you need to tell them, Willie.*" He told me later that freed him up to go on stage and be himself and tell his incredible story of brokenness and recovery. As Willie talked that day, I was amazed at his honesty, openness, and vulnerability. I was shocked, he was telling everyone what a failure he had been, and he didn't seem humiliated by it. In fact, he had a gleam in his eye like he knew something about everyone out there in the audience that they didn't know about themselves.

I thought, "*If I ever got up there and told of my struggles like that, I'd be run out of town!*" Willie finished his talk and told the church we were starting a class to help people either struggling themselves or who have a loved one struggling with addiction. Willie and I went to the back of the church to shake hands as was the custom in those days. I was stunned to see people genuinely moved! Most congregants gave Willie a big hug, several had tears streaming down their faces, most committed to pray for the ministry effort, and all were saying God bless you Willie P! This was so counter-intuitive to me; I couldn't get my mind around it.

However, the real test would be the following week. To everyone's amazement, the first week of the new class twenty-six people came! Willie's honesty tapped something in our congregation they had never seen before. Willie's recovery gave them hope there may be help for them or their loved one. Twenty-six Baptists, who probably never admitted to a struggle in their lives, humbled themselves and went into a room to say we need help and don't have a clue where to start. We learned of pillars in the church that had addicted children but had been suffering in silence because of the shame and sense of failure as parents.

I was confused. I thought being adequate was being perceived as successful, talented, being able to prepare and preach a Bible message. I thought being sufficient was all about how big I could grow the church. I thought being adequate was I didn't ever fail. My pride and fear of being exposed kept me trapped in a fictitious world that operated from one of the outer protective layers I wrote about earlier. But Willie talked to us with no notes and no protective layers. He only shared what was in his broken core and how God met him at that place of woundedness and brought healing. He seemed to have no shame, just gratitude. Unlike what I thought would happen people were drawn to Willie's humility and transparency. His story birthed hope in the audience. His story moved people toward wanting to see their lives changed for the better too. In fact, that morning the resulting ministry shaped the entire future ministry of our church. We developed a core value that said, "We will love you however you come through the doors, and we exist to love people back to life!"

It has taken me years to unravel what transpired in those days of our recovery program. When Jesus Christ comes into our lives and begins the transforming process, every change that is made prepares us to be sufficient in that area to help another. Adequacy has nothing to do with polish and perfection instead it has everything to do with honesty, humility, and hope. Jesus was honest, humble and brought hope to others in his earthly time and people were drawn to him. Jesus didn't come to make us religious practitioners; he came to redeem and use our broken lives.

Willie P has his secrets out in the open for the world to see and people seek him out for help. I've been in the vehicle with Willie when a presidential candidate called him for help with his addicted son! Yes, I mean a national figure, who was running for the White House, called Willie P a roofer and recovering addict for help! It reminds me of when Nicodemus came to Jesus at night for help![25]

Jesus has come to redeem our core wounding for his purposes. He has come to replace our brokenness with a sense of being loved, accepted and adequate for whatever He wants us to do. He makes us suitable and actually can make us experts in the arena that was once our greatest shame! Redemption is a fantastic thing! The most adequate you and I will ever be is when we have taken this journey to our core and allow Jesus to redeem all the broken places. When that happens, we will see the results in the next chapter as we investigate the adventures and impact that will be coming our way.

CHAPTER THIRTEEN
REDEEMED BROKENNESS;
PLATFORM FOR EFFECTIVE
MINISTRY

Connecting with others in a way that makes them feel understood and valued is key to life and the basis of building trust and loyalty and from that base, everything else works.[26] When all the protective layers are stripped away; when we are humbled, exposed, broken but then redeemed, we are now in a place that connection with others is possible.

Earlier I wrote about Jesus encounter with the Samaritan Woman at the well. He cut through her religious and social protective layers and went right to her core shame and wounding, [17] *"I don't have a husband," the woman replied. Jesus said, "You're right! You don't have a husband—[18] for you have had five husbands, and you aren't even married to the man you're living with now. You certainly spoke the truth!"* [27] After Jesus revealed himself to her as the Messiah, most scholars believe she responded positively to that message. When redemption takes place, the same areas that were her greatest shame became the platform for effective ministry. [28] *The woman left her water jar beside the well and ran back to the village, telling everyone,* [29] *"Come and see a man who told me everything I ever did! Could he possibly be the Messiah?"* [30] *So the people came streaming from the village to see him.* [28]

Two things strike me from this passage. First, the woman runs back to her town proclaiming her amazement about someone who knew all her failures. What that tells me is, Jesus didn't make her feel condemned for her failure but redeemed her from them and gave her hope life would be different moving forward. Second, people in her town knew of this woman. They knew her history. Her honesty and excitement about what had transpired in her interaction with Jesus was believable. The town outcast through her transformation now has enough influence operating from her broken but redeemed core that the town's people came in mass to see Jesus. That is a useful connection with people that only happens when we have connected with our brokenness and minister from that place.

The shame and guilt we carry and work so hard to hide; the public image we work so hard to portray keeps us from effectively connecting with others. The pious platitudes and religious clichés may roll off our tongues; the advice we offer to others may be the truth, but the honest connection cannot take place. Effective ministry is not possible. Like the Pharisees of old, that type of ministry is just laying impossible religious demands on the backs of people rather than effective ministry setting captives free.

Back to the Sunday when Willie P stood before the congregation and vulnerably shared his story from a redeemed core, let's dissect what took place. Usually, at church, we are expecting to hear a sermon. Sermons are mostly delivered in a "preaching" style of communication. The "preaching" style means the person delivering the message is an authority who is teaching the listeners what God expects from their lives.

Much preaching is comprised of explaining what a biblical text means and then an application to show the congregants how to live it out. In preaching courses, I was taught to use direct language for more impact such as, "*You must, or you should.*" My professor said to include yourself in the mandate by saying, "*We must or we should,*" only watered down the message! From experience, I've discovered the "preaching" style causes the audience to put up their defenses to block the message.

When Willie stood before the church and told his story of how the Lord redeemed his shame and helped him overcome his addictions. The message came from an authentic place rather than a fabricated image. Like it or not, the audience couldn't keep the message from going straight to their wounded core. Unlike the preacher's message that goes from his head to the audience's head, Willie's message went from his heart to our hearts. Our defenses all were dropped as the story penetrated to the depths. There was nothing to defend because Willie wasn't preaching at us to do anything; he only shared his story from a redeemed core. Once a message connects and goes through all the protective layers and pierces the heart, God's Spirit will begin the transformation process in the audience as well. People are emboldened when they hear the truth and now know they are not suffering alone. They will want to hear more not less from that person. Hope is kindled. Healing seems possible. Redemption is within reach.

Not everyone has such a dramatic story as Willie. So, what about those who don't? What about a person who is in ministry and has to teach every week? No one wants to hear the same story over and over again. Here is what I have done with this concept. I not only have a big story of redemption to share on special occasions to a new audience, but I have many little stories of redemption that I share weekly. I lead a men's ministry and teach once a week.

I made a vow to the Lord and to my men that goes like this. "*Lord, I will teach the men whatever you teach me, no matter how humbling.*" This requires me to maintain a relationship with the

Lord in a dynamic way so when Monday comes, I have something fresh to share with the men. Then, I stand before them and say, *"Men, here is what the Lord is teaching me this week."* I'm not preaching at them. I don't tell them they have to do anything. I simply tell my story of the Lord's teaching to me. I share how some Scripture or principle has exposed me in some area that needs correction or instruction. Their defenses are down. They listen intently, okay, most of the time they listen. God works! Transformation happens. Core wounds are visited, exposed, healed and redeemed. Almost weekly, a man will say, *"Wow, when you were telling your story tonight, it was my story too."* People are eager to listen when you tell on yourself; they don't want to hear it when you aim your talk at them!

Most evangelism classes offered at church attempt to give the students some canned approach to share the gospel message. What if instead, we taught people what it looks like to have a growing and vital relationship with Jesus Christ and share with others what God has given them? I will talk more about this concept in the very last chapter of this book.

Some would say this approach really won't work, especially for pastors who have to teach weekly to multiple groups of people. Wayne Cordeiro, the pastor of New Hope Church in Honolulu, has approximately 14,500 members. I read where he leads multiple groups of people throughout the week. His approach is to read the Bible and record in a journal what God is teaching him through the passage. Then, rather than preparing multiple lessons, he shares with each group what God is showing him. He has also written a book titled, The Divine Mentor that illustrates this concept.

I believe this approach to ministry will bear the most fruit, will have the most credibility and keeps the focus on the Lord. It bears fruit because people get real about the deep wounds and struggles of their lives. It is credible because the people who share, when coming from a place of brokenness and humility are believable. People are astute enough to sense when someone is telling the truth, and it is attractive. It is credible also because the listener often realizes later that the story, they heard applies to them. Rather than being preached at them, the truth works like a Trojan Horse, getting by all the defenses and springing up from deep within.

The focus stays on the Lord because what he shows me about myself humbles me. In retelling what I'm learning from him, it exalts his truth and work and shows that I'm still a work in progress. The truth is, God is at work to conform us to the image of Jesus Christ. That will not be accomplished till we see him.[29] Between that day and my present status, God will continue this transforming process.[30] As long as we stay open and continue to grow, we have a fresh and vital message to share.

The Bible teaches, *"Preach the Word."*[31] How then does this concept line up with that passage? My answer would have multiple components. The approach I am advocating keeps the person who is sharing what they are learning from being a hypocrite. Also, this method is teaching the word of God but in an incarnational approach. Finally, this system makes the vital teaching of Scripture available to all Christ followers!

When as a Christian leader I need to pump out one or more messages on a weekly basis, it becomes easy to start teaching truth from the pages of Scripture that have not impacted me personally. I end up showing you what the Bible says you should do when I know I haven't applied it to my own life. When I commit to teaching you only what I am learning, that won't happen.

Incarnation is the concept of God's life living in me, similar to how God became flesh in the person of Jesus. Don't take this wrong, but the Bible is paper and ink until those words are brought to life by the Spirit of God in the experience of a person. When through the activity of God's Spirit and His Word in my life, real redemption and life change happen. Sharing that life begets life in you too.

Finally, you don't need a degree in theology to lead others with this model. All you need is a relationship with Jesus. The length of time you have known him is not nearly as significant as having your heart open. I believe your journey to the core equips you to be a minister more than a degree from the most exceptional seminary.

Every year at our men's retreat I ask some of the guys who have come to the group and have been broken, humbled and redeemed to share their story. I always get an argument! *"I'm not a public speaker!" "I don't know how to do a talk."* Here is what I ask of them. Don't make a bunch of notes. Don't fret over what to say. Focus on what the Lord is teaching you and tell us your story. Then I watch and listen to a man stand in front of a group of peers and share how God showed him an area of his life that needed work. He will share the argument he had with the Lord and how finally surrender came and the result. It moves me to see the impact on the other men.

I've watched men whose wives have left their marriage come to see their part in the demise of their marriage and humbly share that through tears. I've watched another share how God convinced him, his habit with pornography needed to stop. Man after man, issue after issue, life-change, redeemed cores and new platforms for ministry continue to transpire and inspire This is the real work Jesus came to accomplish, and it is so powerful, well, the enemy fears people whose platform of ministry is their redeemed core!

CHAPTER FOURTEEN
THE ENEMY FEARS YOU!

I remember reading through <u>Wild at Heart</u>, John Eldredge's work for the second time. One line stuck out to me, and I remember exactly where it was on the page of the book. Eldredge was talking about Satan's strategies against us, and he dropped this line, "*Satan will try to get you to agree with intimidation because **he fears you.***"[32] I believe the enemy does fear you and me; when we are no longer playing the church game. He fears us when we have taken the journey to the core and faced our worst. He no longer has all his best weapons against us like shame, secrecy, guilt, bitterness and the feelings of inadequacy. He fears the captive who has been set free. What happens when people everywhere are telling their authentic stories of brokenness and redemption? What happens when others who have been lurking in the shadows of their shame are given inspiration and hope through the retelling of the redemptive stories? No wonder Satan fears you!

When Willie and I started the recovery ministry, our church was still a suit and tie kind of place. This was in the early 1990s. We were not reaching many people who didn't have some church background. Willie told me, "*Now some of the people who come to this class have never been to church, and they may have tattoos and no teeth, and they certainly won't have a suit.*" Can you imagine how heaven rejoiced and Satan trembled when seeing what was transpiring in our group?

Willie has an extensive network of friends and acquaintances from all walks of life. It was amazing to me the number of men he brought to me who needed the Lord and some healing in their lives. We were quite the team. I remember one big 270 lb. gruff and ruff man who came to our class. His name was Richard. He was a beast! He was big, buff and bad. He could hit a softball or golf ball a mile. He was a scary kind of guy with a very intimidating exterior.

We took a bunch of guys on men's retreat, and Richard went. When we got back at our cabin, we put a chair in the middle of the room and one by one, each man sat in it, and all the other guys got around them and prayed for them individually. As a man got in the chair, we ask if he had anything particular, for which we could pray for him. Many began to open up and share some more in-depth stuff. It was a very emotional time.

After Richard's time in the chair, he wanted to talk to me privately. He opened up and cried like a baby. He told me stories of the abuse he endured as a child, being held underwater in a bathtub by his dad and other traumatic events. He said how afraid he was so because of his size he could act big and bad but that inside he was just a little boy who felt backed into the corner by life. I will never forget the night I baptized Richard because he was the biggest guy I ever baptized. I am 5'8" and about 150 lbs. Richard was 6'2" and about 270! He made quite a wave, but we both came up out of the water!

What I didn't know previously was Richard was known as the "King of Churchland." He was involved in all kinds of things in his town and was feared. You didn't cross him and not pay the price. The redeemed Richard was so different. He was humble, soft-spoken a genuinely good man. When Richard began to let other people know he was a Christian and was attending our church can you imagine? When Richard would tell his story, which he did one Easter Sunday Morning to a packed house at church good things happen. As much as people feared the old Richard, Satan feared a broken and redeemed Richard!

When I look at the men who gather on Monday Nights, I see what a powerful tool in God's hands they will be once the Lord does what He does in their lives. The men who are the most beat up and beat down will be the most potent tools in God's hands once they surrender and work through their pain and addictions. What the enemy means to destroy our Heavenly Father uses to redeem.

I would like to speak into the lives of those who are in a Christian Leadership role. You may have achieved a powerful position of leadership but have not done the hard work I'm writing about here. We prefer to let the past be the past. We hide behind religious clichés like *"Calvary covers it all."* We also prefer to project an image of having our stuff together. The rate of men and women leaving ministry annually due to some moral collapse is all the evidence I need.

Most in ministry will not do the hard work to become spiritually and emotionally healthy until they are forced to do so. One of my purposes is to help leadership teams to learn about these concepts before the train wrecks rather than after! Here is what I experience going to church and watching the productions. I experience a lack of humility. I experience very little emotional connection between the speaker, worship leaders, and audience. I hear many good Bible truths taught but from the speaker's head to my head. I often see the glaring inconsistency between what the speaker says and what he does.

I experience watching leaders struggle with the same issues for years while teaching the congregation we should have victory in Jesus. I experience dysfunctional leadership with little interaction and communication on the team. I hear many entertaining messages but very few that touch me emotionally and spiritually enough to cause inspiration to change anything. There is a form of godliness, but there is a lack of power. Satan does not fear these leaders as they are, but he does fear what they could become!

One of the most amazing truths in all of life is how Satan attempts to destroy and thinks he has won, but God intervenes and redeems a life and ends up using an apparent tragedy for good. The clearest example of this truth is found in the life of Jesus. The crowd turned against him. One week prior they were celebrating him coming to town on what we know as Palm Sunday. The next week, he is falsely arrested, mocked, tried, convicted and crucified. Tony Campolo, is professor emeritus of sociology at Eastern University and one of his best-known talks is titled, "Its Friday but Sunday's Comin."

In his message, Tony says, *"Its Friday, Jesus is on the cross. The powers of darkness appear to have won. Satan is dancing the jig. But, that's because it's Friday, Sundays a comin!"* What appeared to be Satan's most significant coup d'état ended up being his undoing. One of the greatest evidence of the sovereignty of God is how evil events can be redeemed into a positive life-changing events. Satan thought he eliminated his competitor. Instead, Christ's death for our sin and resurrection to give new life eliminated any chance of a satanic victory. His doom was sealed and our victory won!

Can you picture yourself living through whatever you are facing right now? Satan wants to destroy you, precisely the same way he tried to destroy Jesus. You may be in your own time of trial. Everything in your life may look dark right now. But that's because it's Friday, Sunday's a comin! If you will fully surrender your life and your mess to Jesus, He will redeem you, heal you and help you.

Can you picture yourself broken and humble but full of empathy for others who struggle as you did? Can you imagine Jesus now using you to bring hope and help to others? I can see that for you because I have watched it happen time after time. When you get healed up and are in that place, Satan is foiled once again. Another person he meant to destroy has now become a powerful tool in the hands of God! You can be that person!

PART THREE
LIVING FROM THE CORE

CHAPTER FIFTEEN
WHAT YOU SEE IS ME

One of my favorite definitions of integrity is *"the quality or state of being complete or undivided."*[33] In essence that is what this journey to the core produces in us. It allows us to work through all the layers of protection and all the lies we have believed and to become healthy. It will enable us to come to a place where we can know and be known. This truth allows us to connect at the deepest possible level with others. One of the best ways I've seen this goal illustrated, see next page, is by using the Johari Window.[34] The Johari Window pictures both what we know and don't know about ourselves and what others know and don't know about us. There is a window with four sections. Our level of personal integration will determine the size of each of the four panes. Perfect integration would mean the window has only one pane and it would be the open area. Let me explain. The four quadrants are 1) the open area. This space represents what I know about me and what you know about me. 2) The blind area represents what you know about me that I don't know about me. 3) The hidden area describes what I know about me, and you don't know about me. 4) The unknown area is what neither you nor I know about me. Only God knows what is in the unknown area. Someone just learning about this journey may have many layers built up to where the unknown,

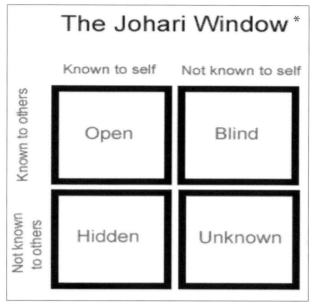

hidden and blind areas may represent a large part of their window. The open area may be quite small because of the tendency to guard against further hurts. A good exercise is to put a percentage in each quadrant that would equal 100%. Based on your perception, how much of you, the real you is open, maybe 30%?

As we grow through this journey, the open area increases and the other areas begin to shrink.

I'd like to define and explain each quadrant to help us along the journey to the core, so ultimately, we can live from the core. The open area grows as you make discoveries and peel back the protective layers. The more aware you are of yourself, and the more you live an authentic, genuine life of integrity (meaning not divided) the more extensive your open area. As you are growing in awareness, the blind area shrinks. As you grasp your redemption and what it means, the hidden field shrinks as well. The open space doesn't necessarily mean everyone knows everything about you. What it does mean is you are growing in understanding yourself, and you have included significant others in the discovery. You have shared what you are learning about yourself with some trusted people. When living this way your life feels more genuine to you and therefore less guarded. You are living more from a redeemed core. When *"What I see is you and what you see is me"* though we may not be privy to all the things each has discovered, someone is, and that frees us to be ourselves around all people.

This whole journey is a lifetime process. This tool is an excellent way to measure how our journey is progressing. The larger the open area, the more we have grown toward the goal.

The blind area is my least favorite. This area is what is evident to others concerning me, but to which I am clueless. This area is water cooler fodder! Gossip finds most its juicy morsels here. All of us have areas of our lives that have been part of us for so long, we are oblivious to them.

I was at a seminar for work on developing sales techniques. I love leadership development stuff; I've read widely and am super engaged. This particular training, I felt the leader was less than I expected. I kept raising my hand and asking questions. I could tell the leader was becoming uncomfortable, but I persisted. I was going to help us get our money's worth out of this training. The teacher started focusing more on the other side of the room, and if I raised my hand, she started ignoring me.

At day's end, I was in the men's room freshening up for the ride home. I looked at myself in the mirror and was questioning why others were not as engaged I was. I reasoned within, maybe they just don't care, or perhaps they don't know as much as I do. At that moment, it was like the Spirit helped me by probing, *"Maybe you are perceived by others as a know it all."*

I asked my immediate supervisor for feedback. He confirmed what the Lord said to me. I even did a Google search for the phrase, know-it-all. When I opened the first article, my picture was there!

Not really, but the article did describe me. I had to find contact information on the teacher and apologize for what I had done to her. The best remedy for the blind area is to seek honest feedback from others. You will need to initiate permitting people to tell you the truth. I would rather have a friend talk to me about less than becoming things in my life than to have others talk behind my back.

The hidden area is my closet of secrets. These are things that I fear if you knew about me you wouldn't want to associate with me. They may be past failures or current struggles. The more we move through the concept of this book, all the discoveries of the journey, experiencing the redeeming of our core and now free to live an open life using all for good, the more the hidden area will shrink. The things that were once hidden, the broken pieces of our lives when redeemed become our platform for ministry. They once held us in shame, now humbled we use them to help set other captives free. The remedy for the hidden area is a healthy and growing relationship with the Lord and your willingness to confess your faults to him and another human being.[35]

The unknown area I call the abyss! I believe many of the things in the unknown area are brought to awareness through this journey. The Lord will reveal things that have been outside your consciousness. He will show you patterns of relating and behavior that you absorbed through your upbringing and early development that you couldn't see.

There may always be some mysteries in this area that will help propel your journey all the way to the end of your life. There is nothing in the unknown area that isn't known by God. The remedy to shrink this area is to trust in his time and when you are ready; he will reveal to you the more profound things that will move you to the next level of freedom, growth, and usefulness. The ultimate objective is one big picture window that is open and free. As you walk toward that goal, living from the core means you can say with integrity, *"What you see is me."*

CHAPTER SIXTEEN
YOUR LAST VOTE

Church government has been a controversial issue over the years. The question is, who has the authority to make decisions for the church organization. Throughout church history, there have been several forms of government, and my purpose is not to bore you with all that.

Among evangelical churches, there are two predominant concepts. This understanding will help you grasp what this living from the core will require of you. Many churches are *"congregational rule."* This idea means leaders cannot make decisions without a congregational vote of approval. It places the decision-making power in the majority of the congregants. Different churches take this to different lengths, but I have personally seen congregational votes taken on whether the walls of a classroom could be painted.

The second variation of church government moves the decision-making ability to a team of leaders. It is usually a group of people called Elders whose role is to oversee the ministry. The church may still have limited voting power such as approving the annual budget, agreeing on a building program and other major decisions.

The last vote our congregation took was a vote to surrender the reigns of decision making over to our elders. Therefore, their last vote was to say in theory; we will trust someone else who has more experience, more knowledge of the issues and the wellbeing of the whole ministry at heart.

How does church government have anything to do with living from the core? To live from the core, we must make our last vote to surrender to the word, ways and work of God in our lives. We give up our right to vote! I heard a radio personality say one time there were many decisions she was free not to make because her faith already made them for her. She was saying because I ascribe to the Jewish Faith and its teachings, I've committed to do what the faith teaches. Therefore, I don't struggle with some decisions rather see what our faith teaches how I should respond and then just do it.

To live a healthy, integrated life from the core, we will need to take our last vote. I vote to surrender myself to the Lord and his word and work in my life. We will actively pursue knowing Him and the truth, so we can then live out what he teaches.[36] Most the damage in my life has come by me taking willful control of my life. When I take control, it means the man who is created in God's image, who is loved unconditionally, who has been adopted by God and who has been given eternal significance; will get buried under layers of hurt and protection! I can see the unhealthy patterns I master when I'm in control. I know where my best thinking has gotten me. Therefore, with eyes wide open, it makes perfect sense for me to surrender my life, my decisions and my future to God.

A life lived from a redeemed core is counter-intuitive. I share things most people hide and other people get better. I tell my worst and people are drawn to me more. I believe I'm more spiritual than ever, but those far from God are more comfortable in my presence. I prepare less when I have the opportunity to share or preach, but God uses what I say more than when my finest crafted messages came from a surface layer of protection. With nothing to hide, I have more energy to invest in life, more peace that puts me and others at ease. A life lived from the redeemed core is the natural outcome of the journey. It is the fruit of God's work to heal us and set us free to live for him.

The analogy of a congregations' last vote, is called surrendering to Jesus for the individual Christian. That is a once and for all decision. The decision though requires daily affirming of that choice. No one does this perfectly! The best of the best is still in the process of being conformed to be like Jesus. One thing that helps me is to start my day with the following prayer.

"Father, I humble myself before you today. You are everything, and you have everything I need. I surrender to you for these twenty-four hours. My only prayer is to know your will and have the power to carry it out. Allow me to serve someone today with no expectation of return. I'm available to share my story any time you need me."

CHAPTER SEVENTEEN
LEARNING TO LOVE

O ver this decade of healing, learning and growing, I have read widely and listened to many messages from the country's best teachers. I've come to appreciate the teaching style of Andy Stanley.[37] I have always struggled with, *"Don't be selfish; don't try to impress others. Be humble, thinking of others as better than yourselves."*[38] I've always prided myself on being a student and feeling like I know why I believe what I do. The truth is, I could use what I know to wiggle out of many things I should have done for the sake of love. While a person has so much buried pain, so many protective layers while believing the lies and not knowing the truth, it is difficult to look beyond your own life.

For a time in the mornings, I would watch Andy Stanley sermons online.[39] There was a series of messages entitled, *"Christian."* At this point, I had done all the work I've written about in the early chapters, and now it seemed the Lord was rebuilding my life on the redeemed core. This series of messages should be a top priority for all Christians to hear. For me, the timing was perfect. I had cleared through all the clutter and was ready to learn a new way.

The messages taught that in the early church the one thing that marked Christians was the love of Christ working in and through them. Jesus didn't tell his followers *"The world will know you are my followers because you have your doctrine straight."*[40] Andy pointed out how through church history during plagues and the like, when everyone else was running out of the cities for fear of their lives; Christians ran in to care for the sick. Andy asked a question during this series that will not let me alone. *"What would love require of me in this situation?"* When he first asked that question it hit me right in the heart. It went through my head continually for days.

I travel some for my day job for a natural gas utility. I had been gone for several days, and I'm almost home, and it is supper time. Within a block of home, I see a senior man and a young girl attempting to change a flat tire. I could see they were struggling some, but I wanted to get home. I tried to look away! The question comes to my mind, *"What would love require in this situation."* My decision was made. I helped them change their tire. It only took a few minutes, and I still was home for dinner with Gayle. Asking and answering that question has shined a light on which path to choose in many situations since.

I heard a young lady speak at the Global Leadership Summit produced by the Willow Creek Association. Her name is Pranitha Timothy.[41] When I heard this soft-spoken, huge-hearted lady share how she had risked her life to help people who are being trafficked, something resonated deep within my spirit. I saw in her a surrender, love, compassion, and courage that I have never experienced. It appeared she had given the Lord control of her life and she was willing to do whatever he asked, and she loved and trusted him. I've only encountered a few people in my life that have impacted me with that same spirit. It is a beautiful thing. One of the first times I sensed this same humble, loving spirit was the previous year at the same conference.

A lady in a flowing white covering came before the crowd. Humility leaked from her every pour. She bowed in humility and asked God to take and use her life. Mama Maggie Gobran, this humble saint had left a life of teaching science at the American University in Cairo to spend twenty years serving the children of the Zabbaleen. This is an impoverished community that lives among the garbage slums of Cairo. Amid all the hotshot American preachers and business leaders sharing their excellent stuff with us, Mama was a spirit so rare the entire crowd was deeply touched. She possessed a spirit of love and sacrifice I have never seen in the American Church. I am not saying it isn't present; I've just never seen it. Her talk but even more her demeanor left a mark on me. I'm not even sure about all either ladies' theology but this I know I saw Jesus in them more clearly than ever in anyone, and I want to be more like Him because of them!

During this phase of rebuilding "*The Cure,*"[42] was published. I don't read much fiction, but I have read other works by the same authors and have found their work refreshing. This book was going to be used by God to help in my rebuilding. I'm not going to rewrite the book here but to say it was all about living "*In the room of grace.*"

After reading the book, I was out for a run. I remember exactly where I was when this insight came to me. I was running down a bridge on PGA Blvd that goes over I-95 in Palm Beach Gardens, FL. I saw clearly in my head, the Lord in the room of grace and I was there with him. I was thinking about all he has done for me. I was thinking how great his love for me is. I was thinking about how amazing he could forgive me for everything I've ever done and treated me like I was already perfected. I began to sing "*Amazing Grace how sweet the sound that saved a wretch like me. . .*" I was having a real encounter with the Lord. It seemed he was saying to me this grace is amazing, isn't it? Doesn't it feel great to be here in this room with me?

Then I sensed him say, *now that you understand what grace feels like do you think there is room in here for your wife, Gayle? Do you think you can invite her into this room of grace? Can you see her how I see you;*

imperfect yet perfect, flawed but in the process, my daughter who is loved and forgiven, just as you are. With a heart full of love and understanding, I said, "Yes, *there is room here for her!*" The Lord continued to probe, "*Since you understand the concept and now have made room here for Gayle, how about all your kids? Now, how about the people you work with? How about people at church?*"

By the time he was done with me, I saw that I was to make room for everyone in the world in the room of grace. It should be where and how I live my life. Later that day, driving through the city streets of West Palm Beach, a homeless man was begging, holding his cardboard sign. "*Do you have space in the room of grace for him?*" the Spirit probed. Honestly, having grasped the concept of grace myself, it was effortless for me to answer, "*Yes Lord, there is plenty of room for him too.*" My heart welled up with compassion for the man, and I sensed a real love for the man. I decided I would take out a mortgage and buy him a home, just kidding! But for all who know me, hearing me say what I did is a huge breakthrough.

I'm slowly learning at the core of every human there is a person created in the image of God, who is loved with an everlasting love by God. Those truths are buried deeply through sin, hurt and many protective layers. Living from the core means I have taken the long journey to my core and since I have been redeemed; I can perceive every human has amazing potential. I believe every person who lives from this redeemed core will be able to see people through the eyes of grace and love. Others will identify us as Christ-followers because we have an overflowing love for people and a humble spirit.

So, I've got the question ringing in my ears, "*What does love require of me in this situation,*" and I've seen modeled in the two ladies at Willow Creek, the humblest spirit of Christ Likeness ever. I am left with choices will I practice what I've seen and heard. I'm also learning there needs to be another skill learned! We will take that up in the next chapter.

CHAPTER EIGHTEEN
LEARNING TO LISTEN

In my early Christian Life, I had developed a healthy relationship with the Lord through reading his word and spending regular large doses of time with him. I wanted to know and do what he wanted. I had learned and taught others to listen for his promptings.

During Bible College, I read a book titled, "*Decision Making and the Will of God*" by Gary Friesen. Friesen presents in his book that God leads the believer through his word, and if his word doesn't say explicitly what to do, then we are free to use our best wisdom to determine our path. He also argues that God does not have a specific will for each. I digested that book and felt a sense of relief. I would guess Dr. Friesen may not agree with my conclusion, but I began at that point not to worry so much about hearing the promptings from God. Friesen did write there is no way anyone could prove those leadings was really from God. Something changed in me at that time, and it wasn't for the best.

I've had some times over the years when I would return to my roots and connect with the Lord in a way that I sensed him speaking to me. He has taught me so many things through this spiritual connection; I'm not sure how I could ever have doubted. I can't argue from science, but I can argue from experience that God still speaks to and prompts his children. I believe it usually is to make a general truth of Scripture apply to a specific situation or to prompt us to an act of service. He is the head, and we are the body. It only makes sense he could nudge us when he needs us to be his hands, feet, ears or mouthpiece.

A few years ago, one of my heroes of the faith, Bill Hybels wrote a book titled, "*The Power of the Whisper.*" Bill goes through situation after situation where the course of his whole Christian Journey has been directed by those inner promptings of the spirit of God. His whole calling, the establishment of The Willow Creek Community Church, the development of the Willow Creek Association and their worldwide influence are all attributed by Hybels as the result of obedience to the divine whisper.

I was away on a business trip and reading that book. It had been too long since I heard from God. I was going through this journey to my core. Sometimes the journey was so hard. I uncovered so much pain; I just wanted to escape it. When I was on the road, I would often take the edge off with an extra glass of wine with dinner. I was in West Palm Beach, FL staying in a downtown hotel. I had dinner, and I was reading Hybels book.

The next morning, I was going out for my typical 5-6-mile run. It was 6 AM as I headed out and I was praying, "*Lord, that book has stirred my heart. It has been a long time since I've heard from you. Would you talk to me today? Would you let me know you are still there?* I left the hotel and headed over the bridge on the intercoastal waterway that goes to Palm Beach proper. Palm Beach is one of the wealthiest places in our country. There is a running/walking trail that follows the intercoastal to the next bridge north and makes a very nice three-mile loop. I would usually run this loop twice. I was in a spiritual place at this time best described as, "*I don't care too much anymore.*" I was pretty much convinced I was done. I would never be overly useful to the Lord again.

So, I'm now running up the intercoastal enjoying a beautiful morning, admiring the mansions on my right and the accompanying yachts on my left. I sensed the Lord speak to me. *"If you lived in one of these mansions and owned the yacht that goes with it you wouldn't be happy."* My first thought was, maybe not but it would be fun to try. Like interference on a radio signal, his statements kept interrupting my thoughts. I was running along and looked left to the West Palm Beach skyline. It was still dark, and the buildings were lit. I could see the words; Trump Plaza lit up.

Out of nowhere, *"You wouldn't be happy if you owned that whole city. In fact, if you did own the city and you could walk in any boardroom, and everyone stood in respect of you, it wouldn't be enough."* I thought, wow that is a little harsh, but I know me and thought, after a while, I would be bored with all that. I agreed you are probably right Lord. He was right, and he wasn't done. *"If you owned the city and were respected by every businessman and all the beautiful young girls were willing to give themselves to you, that wouldn't be enough for you either!"* He stopped, but now my mind started rehearsing some scriptures. *"What does it profit a man to gain the whole world and loses his own soul?"*[43]*"Don't lay up for yourselves treasures on earth where moth nor rust can corrupt, and thieves break in and steal."*[44]

I began to think even pastoring a church that was so big all the people could never meet at the same time, speaking to hundreds of thousands would fade in time. Then just as quickly as the interaction began it was done. I was running taking it all in. Thinking about what I heard. I had run quite a while longer and thought the Lord was done, but then I heard a question in my head that wasn't from my thinking. *"Do you know how I know that none of those things would be enough for you?"* I said out loud, *"No Lord, other than you know everything, I'm not sure how you know that."*

He gave me the knockout punch, *"I know because I am the God of the universe, I've created everything. I am everything, and I have everything you will ever need, and you have not been satisfied with me. If you aren't satisfied with the Creator, you will never be able to fully appreciate anything I've created. Nothing I have given you will be enough till I am your everything and I am everything you need."* Honestly, it nearly dropped me to my knees, but I had to agree with him. For weeks I could not shake this encounter from my mind. For weeks and even months, I would start my day by saying, *"You are everything Lord, and you are everything I need. Help me to see all you have given me as gifts from your generosity. I humble myself before you today."*

With the connection reestablished and Friesen's Book out of my mind and heart and Hybels' premise replacing it, I began to expect God to be able to give me promptings when he had something for me to do. The openness to hear the promptings linked with the question *"What does love require of me,"* has been a source of great blessing to me and those I'm prompted to serve. Without the journey to the core described here all the buried clutter in my life kept me focused on me. I wasn't in a place to care that much about anyone else. God's heart is for the whole world and he wants to use Christians in their sphere of influence and beyond to make an impact for good. Living from the core will require a new kind of giving.

CHAPTER NINETEEN
LEARNING TO GIVE

Anyone who has gone to an evangelical church has been taught about giving. In the old days, we were instructed to give your time, treasure and talent. Even recently, I've seen the question asked on Facebook, "*How does a pastor separate his work from his service for the Lord?*" The church so often divides life up into pieces like this. Give a portion of your income to the church, and that makes you a giver. Give a portion of your time to attend services, serve in some capacity and attend a small group, and that makes you a dedicated Christian. Do all the above, and you are in the elite status of the American churchgoer! A person can develop the mentality when those items are checked off the list you have given and sacrificed for the church (not the same as the Lord), and now the rest of your life and stuff is yours to use as you wish.

Since becoming Christians, Gayle and I have given between 10-20% of our income to the church. I have never considered myself a generous giver. I could justify giving to the Lord in the New Testament is primarily through the local church. I felt like I not only did my duty but went beyond. It was easy for me to turn a deaf ear to other needs because I had convinced myself I did what God expected. This is much like the story in the New Testament of the

Pharisee who wouldn't help his parents financially because he said he dedicated his extra money to God![45]

Gayle is a budgeter extraordinaire! I attribute most of our financial freedom to her persistence in managing our finances in a biblical and fiscally responsible way. Finances have caused so many issues in the lives of people. The bottom line on money is one thing, "*Spend less than you make.*" The American version of that principle is as long as your monthly payments are less than what you bring in you are okay. The amount of debt we carry doesn't seem to bother many. The money we spend on interest to use someone else's money is poor stewardship in many cases. One of the things we are learning is when payments and income are nearly the same; it makes it hard to be a generous giver. When I am worried about whether my money will stretch, I do not incline to give you any!

Through managing our money well, we were in a position we could help others, but before this journey, my heart wasn't in the right place to want to become a generous giver. Through the course of the journey, learning to love better and learning to listen better will almost always mean I am learning to give better too! Because God is love and love gives, when a person is in tune with the Lord and hearing his promptings, generous giving will be the natural outcome.

I'm going to tell a couple of stories of what it has looked like to be at the Lord's disposal giving of my money and myself. Our life group had signed up to serve at a local ministry that feeds low income and homeless people. As I stated earlier, the guy on the street with the cardboard sign has never elicited sympathy from me. I always felt like for the most part real homeless people are embarrassed by their situation and know where the shelters and food are but would not stand to beg on the corner.

My view is the people who do the in your face begging have chosen to be homeless. It may be due to addictions or some other choice, but I felt they just didn't want to work. My thought toward them was, *"Get a job bum."*

During our time at the I AM Hope Café; my role was to mingle with the people. We were serving one night in the colder time of the year where temperatures get near freezing at night. The county opens overnight shelters but only if it is predicted to get below freezing. As the people started coming in to get their dinner, I was talking to one man. He told me how this time of the year was more difficult because of the cold. He went in to get his food. This next part is so foreign to me it is why I chose this story. I had a prompting in my spirit, *"Go to Wal-Mart and buy him a tent."* The store was directly across the street from the café. Knowing time was of the essence, I immediately went to the store and picked out a nice tent that would be easy to pack up and carry. The café had blankets and clothes they could give out, but we were told not to give the people any money or items. I've never been much of a rule follower, especially if they don't make sense to me! I got back to the café before the man had left. My truck was parked quite a distance from the café in a parking lot.

When the guy came out, I said, *"There is something in the back of that white pickup truck for you."* I watched him heading to my truck, and I was moved with gratitude. When he got there and looked in the back and saw the tent, he looked back at me and pointed to himself saying, *"Is this for me?"* I only ever saw that guy a couple more times, but I never saw him that he didn't tell me how much that tent meant to him. A strange thing happened to me. I learned something about where your treasure is your heart is.[46] I found myself almost every night at bedtime thinking about this man out there in the cold but in his tent, and I would pray for him to be safe, warm and ultimately to know the Lord and find a better way of life.

What I'm learning about giving is when the Lord prompts it, and I can meet a need directly rather than through an organization my heart is tied to the gift. This giving lesson I'm learning is how I am to live from the core. It is a life lived with a clear conscience, a healthy sense of who I am in Christ and giving that away to others. I need to be connected consistently, so I don't miss the promptings. The promptings won't always be to give money; they could be to give away a spiritual truth I'm learning or to help change a tire. The point is there is no segmentation of life. I am dedicated, not because I do a few things on a church check off list. I am dedicated when I have given my entire life to the Lord to be used at his bidding.

On another occasion, I was in Historic Fernandina Beach, FL on a work trip. I stay at the Hampton Inn on the marina right downtown. There is a set of railroad tracks that run right beside the hotel. This particular trip I had a marina front room which meant the tracks were directly next to the room. I had gone out to dinner and had come back in for the night. Gayle and I prayed together over the telephone. By 10:00 PM I was sound asleep.

I was shaken out of my sleep and sat straight up in the bed thinking we were having an earthquake when I realized it was just a train. I felt a strong prodding in my spirit to get out of bed, get dressed and go across the street to the oldest bar in Florida, The Palace Saloon. I laid back down and tried to go back to sleep, but the wrestling match continued. I sensed again a very strong prodding, and I was in full arguing mode. *"The Lord wouldn't tell me to go to a saloon. I'm tired, I've already been to sleep, and I'm not going out anywhere at this hour of the night."* But the prodding seemed to be relentless.

I finally got up and put on some shorts a t-shirt and flip-flops and went to the pub. As I went into the dimly lit room, I heard a guy singing some live music, I could see there was hardly anyone there, and I just sat at a table near the door by myself. My internal dialogue was, *"What am I doing here? As soon as this guy singing takes a break, I'm going back to bed."*

The singer in just a short time said he was taking a short break. As I was getting ready to make my exit two ladies and a gentleman came in and sat down right next to me. One of the ladies reached her hand out to shake my hand and said, *"My name is Julie, and this is my best friend Heather, and I love the Lord, and I love my husband!"* I said, *"My name is Scott, and I love the Lord, and I love my wife too."*

Julie went on to tell me she was from Colorado and Heather was from South Carolina. She called her husband a rock star for staying home with their two children so she could get away. Julie said, *"I've been going through a rough time."* I said, *"So what is wrong?"* She proceeded to tell me it was really deep. I let her know I had been a pastor for eighteen years and had heard most everything. She started telling me her story when the music started back up.

We stepped outside under the street light on the main street corner in downtown Fernandina Beach. She said, *"I was always the Christian with unshakeable faith. I could encourage my friends when they were struggling and point them toward trusting the Lord with their struggles. Two years ago, my oldest brother killed our other brother, our mom and burnt the family home to the ground. My oldest brother got life in prison only because I went and pleaded for his life believing if he were alive, he would have a chance to repent."* She continued, *"I am not on speaking terms with God. I pray with my kids but I'm faking it. I am so angry and confused, and I just don't know what to do."* She dumped on me for some time. I let her get everything out she needed to. Every once in a while, her friend would stick her head out the door to make sure Julie was okay.

I finally felt she was done and I said let me tell you my story. *"I messed up and lost my life as a pastor. I'm wondering if God is done using me. I was sound asleep in my hotel room when I was awoken and sent to this place, and I didn't know why. But it was because God loves you and he knows exactly where you are and he isn't giving up on you. He has used you to show me he isn't giving up on me either."* She looked at me with tears in her eyes and said, *"For the first time in two years I have a flicker of hope."* She went back to her friend, and I went back to the hotel to bed.

The next morning, I was tired but had a great sense of God's favor on my life. I felt like that encounter was one of the most Christ-like encounters of my life. I felt highly favored that God would trust me with someone he loved who was deeply wounded and running from him. Of all people he tapped me on the shoulder and asked me to represent his love by listening and giving my time and my story. I enrolled that morning and told the Lord anytime, anywhere you need me for an emergency call I am willing.

I've been privileged now to have many stories of hearing the Lord ask me to do something to bless someone else. I am always honored he would ask me, trusting me with being his representative to help one of his kids in need. When the Lord interacts with me directly, whether to teach me some truth or to prompt me to give, those encounters are etched in my memory; I never forget one of them.

Jesus told us how this all works. *"I am the vine, and you are the branches. Remain in me, and I in you and you will bring forth much fruit. For apart from me you can do nothing!"*47

I started this journey being filled with disillusionment, shame, guilt, fear, anger, and bitterness. The real person I was meant to be was buried under so many protective layers, some core sin and lies it just wasn't possible to enjoy life. But Jesus said he came that our lives would be full and overflowing. 48 This healing and healthier life are teaching me to be real, to surrender, to love, to listen, to give and the next chapter will reveal the natural result of these things being added to my life.

CHAPTER TWENTY
LEARNING TO PRAISE

N otice I said learning, not I have learned! This entire book is revealing several areas of life that are in the process not completed. The natural outcome of all I've written to this point is a deeper level of gratitude. Just yesterday a friend, who has been stripped to the core through a loss of work and nearly everything he owned, told me after two weeks back to work he is learning not to take anything for granted. He is grateful for the small blessings of life, and he sees them now. The flip side of learning to praise is living an entitled, self-centered life. When things are going well, I think they should go better. When things are going bad, I wonder why I should have to struggle. There is little opportunity to praise with that mindset. When major progress has been made on this journey, you will find an authentic praise for God from a deeper place.

The contemporary church calls the singing part of the service, "Praise and worship." This reminds me of years ago in the Baptist Church Thursday nights were called, "Visitation." That is when we would go out and visit neighbors, and first-time guests to invite them back. For many, once Thursday Night was done, we were off duty till the following Thursday! Our task to share our faith and reach the world was contained on Thursday Nights.

For many others, the entirety of their Christian life is contained in a couple of hours Sunday morning. Compartmentalizing praise and worship to the music portion of the church service is similar to me. Isn't the speaking part, the giving part all praise and worship too? Isn't my time alone with the Lord when I go for a run, bike ride, day at the beach or reclining on my sofa just as much an opportunity to praise the Lord for his blessing? The answer to all this is dependent on where you are on your journey? If you still are living from the religious protective layer, you won't do any more than you think is required to support the façade. Like every other area until it is coming from the depths of who you are it isn't hitting on much.

There are times now where out of nowhere, I will find myself whispering praise to the Lord for something. There have been some times where I feel my eyes well up with tears as I ponder how good God has been to me. It may be looking at my precious grandchildren or thinking about how special Gayle is to me. It may be something as simple as our little Yorkie, Zoe Boy and his unconditional love and the joy he has brought to our home. I'm finding when what you see is me; I'm more prone to gratitude and praise. When I am in that healthier place, I've also discovered I can enjoy the expressive singing portion of our church service more fully too.

Some indicators for me of where I'm at on the journey, whether I'm getting close to living from a redeemed core or still stuck at some outer layer is spontaneous singing. When spiritual songs and hymns bubble up and come out while I'm in the shower or just driving down the road, that singing lets me know it is well with my soul.

Another way for me to know where I am is what I'm thinking about. When I find myself pondering a spiritual reality or a scripture concept or peeling some additional layer back in my personal life, it is a good indicator I'm in a healthy place.

The best sign for me is sensing a rest in my spirit. When I'm not agitated or anxious, when I'm okay to let you be yourself around me, when I'm not highly irritated by things and when I am at peace with myself, I'm good.

All of these seem to be accurate indicators because Jesus taught that whatever is in our hearts, that is whatever we value will be what comes out of our mouths. Anything coming out of our mouths would naturally have processed through our minds first. So, what we think about, sing about, and talk about are good ways to check the condition of our hearts.[49]

This is part of the journey I'm just growing into, so I don't have much more to say. Each of us is wired differently so your expressions of heartfelt praise may be different from mine. The primary thing I want to convey here is, the praise won't be manufactured it will rise from the depths of your being and be genuine like every other part of your life when you are living from the core. This concept of being real leads me to one final issue I'd like to address. That is the concept of the Christian's testimony.

CHAPTER TWENTY-ONE
YOUR TESTIMONY

The Christian circles I cut my teeth in valued their testimony more than anything else. Your testimony, in their mind, was Jesus Christ's advertisement to the people outside the faith. The goal was to present as perfect a picture as humanly possible. I heard many sermons on how a Christian could ruin their testimony. This concept was used to shame us into following all the guidelines the particular church expected, *"What if some unbeliever saw you having a beer?"* *"What if someone you are trying to reach for Christ saw you in line to go to the movies?"* You can fill in your lines there but what was being said is, *"If you appear to be less than perfect you are hurting your testimony."*

That thinking must be corrected, or we remain powerless when attempting to connect with people in the real world. When we follow that model, we are living in the protective religious layer. While I was in those circles the questions, I listed above had power because my mind was trapped in their system of thinking. After some growth and knowing many people who were outside of the faith, I realized doing those things did not affect them at all! No unchurched person would think a thing about having a beer with me and a healthy conversation about the Lord! No person outside of the church would think twice about seeing me in line at the movies, which is a normal part of most people's life. When I believe those things are wrong for whatever reason and don't do them and then criticize others who do, I am in dangerous territory.

So, what exactly is having a good testimony? My testimony is, Jesus died for all my sin and had risen from the grave to give me new life. Recently when teaching this concept, a man asked, *"Didn't Jesus take care of all this journey stuff and core wounds when I accepted him as my Savior?"* It is a fatal flaw in our understanding not to know that accepting Jesus is only the beginning of the journey and not the end. The new life he has given me has resulted in a lifelong journey of growth. It has enrolled me in a process that will keep going all the way till I die.

My testimony is, thank the Lord for dying in my place and for the changes he is bringing in my life. I can share with you eye-opening lessons; I can share with you areas I'm working on, and I can share with you, I know I still have blind spots I'm not aware of yet. It isn't about being perfect; it is about being in the process and progressing. It is being able to say, I am not what I used to be, but I am not what I will be either. There will never be a time in this life when you can say, *"I'm done growing; I've got this thing."* Our testimony is Christ paid for all my junk, and he is my trainer prodding me toward becoming more like him.

In the early days of my faith journey, Gayle and I were members of an Independent, Fundamental, King James only, Baptist Church. The church believed it was wrong to drink any alcohol, use any tobacco product, go to a movie theater, play cards, for a man's hair to be over his ears and preferred women wear skirts or culottes rather than slacks. They also believed any version of the Bible other than the KJV was a perversion. Any music with a rock beat, even if it had Christian lyrics was of the devil. They had standards for how women should dress in almost every venue. They also felt going to the beach or "mixed bathing," as it was called, was a sin. "Mixed bathing" was what they called swimming in the same pool or ocean with people of the opposite sex. Dancing is also forbidden, even to the point for some there was no first dance at a wedding!

Violating any of the above standards meant your "Testimony" was in jeopardy! By the way, there are still small pockets of Christians who would hold to most the above standards. There are a few colleges around the country that would espouse these views and train others to do ministry with that mindset. Most these people are living their lives from the religious protective layer and don't realize it.

To illustrate how strongly these beliefs are held; I have a couple of stories. Our church would allow our ladies to wear jeans when they were playing on our church softball team. We would only play in a league with like-minded churches. Our girls' team was playing against another girls' team from a church across town. The other team's girls wore culottes to play. Culottes for the uninitiated are like loose fitting shorts (to the knee of course), or as a skirt with legs. Only someone blinded by their religion would think culottes are more modest than jeans for playing softball! So, our girls were beating the culottes off the other team when their pastor came up to me. He said, *"Your girls are ruining the testimony of our churches in the community by wearing those pants to play softball."*

One other story comes to mind on this topic. Our teens were going to go away to a youth camp at a nearby Bible College. We had a very serious and somber meeting one night because our pastor found out they were going to be using the New International Version of the Bible. The camp's thinking was it is much easier for the kids to understand. Our church decided we would forbid the kids from attending the camp and write a letter of disapproval and revoke of any support of that college because of their "liberal" position on Bible versions. Our pastor and church felt quite pleased that we maintained our good "Testimony" in the community by taking this stand.

I read these things now and feel the same anger Jesus expressed in his encounters with the Pharisees of his day.[50] The problem with ancient and modern Pharisees isn't their lack of zeal or their lack of commitment; it is their misguided thinking. The problem is thinking somehow their performance is more important than the gospel of grace. The issue is thinking my performance rather than his power is what attracts others.

I have experienced both, thinking my testimony was me looking perfect now knowing my testimony is Jesus Christ has rescued me and is continually shaping my life. The first, I was living a lie from the outer protective layers, and I was an island. I never shared life at a real level with others. I feared I'd be rejected from the church club if they knew my struggles. The response from those outside the church wasn't too great either. They would ask, so what significant changes have you made? I'd say, "*I got a haircut, and I don't drink, smoke or chew or run with girls that do.*" No one ever responded, "*I want what you have!*"

The second approach is humble, vulnerable and attractive. I can share how I was living life for myself when I heard the gospel message. I fearfully opened my life to the work of Jesus. Through my relationship with him, he has been taking me on this journey. He is opening my eyes to one discovery after another. I can't imagine going more than a week or two without having some new lesson he is showing me. That is what I share. I've come to know the Lord and here is what I am learning right now. That is my testimony. Not how good I am rather He's got me and here is my latest life lesson. The response to this approach has been incredible. People probe, ask questions and want to hear more. They resonate with the issues I'm learning about. It is a Christ-like, winsome approach.

As you journey to the core, come to accept the redeeming of the core wounding and begin living from that healthier place you will always have a fresh story to tell. That is your testimony! This is your life; a life lived from the redeemed core!

CONCLUSION

The Lord has a fantastic way of working with each of us as individuals. He is fully capable of taking you on your journey to the core. It is like he has an individual educational plan for each of us and unfolds it only as we are willing to cooperate with him. Real life change is a process, and layers peel over time. This writing represents seventeen years of my life and more specifically the time since <u>Connecting the Dots</u> was published in 2007. So, these discoveries unfold over time.

Jesus never taught a systematic theology class; His method was to invite people to follow him. Through following him and learning to hone in on that still small voice, our inner life grows stronger and more people benefit from our existence.

I work for a utility company and help our customers learn about reducing their energy costs. I go to people's homes when they have high bills and attempt to determine the cause and solution. One morning I was scheduled to do an energy audit in West Palm Beach, Florida. In my quiet time that morning, I surrendered and asked the Lord to allow me to serve someone that day. When I got to the home, there was an Indian Woman with two children with the front door wide open. I learned their air conditioner was not working. The boys followed me around as I did my work. When I was leaving the lady said, I know my air conditioner has a small leak. I just can't find an air conditioning service company to put freon in it.

They all want to sell me a new one, and I don't have the money. She told me last year, her husband had a friend who put the refrigerant in their unit, and it lasted all summer. I said, why doesn't your husband call him again. She told me her husband became ill a few months ago. He went to the hospital and was dead within two weeks. He was only 42 years of age.

As I was leaving, I felt bad for them. It was 95° outside and no air conditioning. I was walking to my car when I sensed the Lord say, didn't you ask me for someone to serve today? Do you need a road sign? I went to my car and called another employee to get the name of a company who would charge the ladies air conditioner. I went back into the home with a name and number of a contractor who would service her system without trying to sell her a new one. She thanked me and said when she could afford it, she would call them. I said okay and felt like I did all I could.

On my way to the car, I was feeling good about helping the lady, when the Lord interrupted my moment of celebrating with a request. I want you to call that company, schedule an appointment and give them your credit card information to pay for it. I'm not usually one who is going to give money to a total stranger. I argued slightly but did what I believed the Lord ask of me. I called the contractor and told them the plan. He said he would get by the home that day by 4:00 pm. He said he would call me to settle up the bill when he was done.

I went back to the door and shared with the lady what was taking place. She is a woman of the Hindu Faith. When I told her, I would pay for it; she began to cry. She said, why would you do something like this for a total stranger. I told her I am a Christian; I asked God for opportunities to serve him, He answered by making me aware of her need. I'm just doing what the Lord asked me to do. She was overwhelmed with gratitude.

I never heard from the contractor. I called the homeowner, and she told me the guy came and fixed her air conditioner and was moved by the story enough to give her a significantly discounted cost. She had the money to pay. I felt disappointed I wasn't able to bless this widow and her boys by paying, but I was willing and obedient to what God asked of me.

Jesus calls us to follow him! He will take you on a life-long journey of growth, adventure and opportunity. When we stay in that close relationship, our lives will become personally more satisfying and make a positive difference in our sphere of influence. I know of no better way to live my life than from a redeemed core following Jesus!

APPENDIX A
KNOWING JESUS

This entire journey is hinged on knowing the Tour Guide! This isn't a self-help manual or a guide to help you make self-improvement. This is a discipleship manual on knowing Jesus and allowing him to guide you on this journey. He knows you perfectly. He knows where the low hanging fruit is in your life. He knows what immediate changes will bring the most benefit. He knows you better than anyone else. The key though is that you know Him! In John 17:3, Jesus said, *"This is the way to have eternal life- to **know you**, the true God and Jesus Christ."* True Christianity is about God and you being in a relationship. In many ways, it is a loving, mentoring relationship. He knows you perfectly, being a Christian means you are getting to know him. So then, how can someone know God?

When you come to know you need help, you need to be forgiven, and you need your life to be different you are ready to make his introduction. When Jesus came to earth and then died on the cross, it was to make this relationship possible. He paid for all our bad stuff so it can be taken away from us clearing the way for us to be in a relationship with a holy God. When Jesus rose from the grave, it was the Father's seal of approval the payment was made in full. Now, because Jesus is alive, you can have a spiritual relationship with him. He will communicate with you through the Bible and even through his spirit. The promptings his spirit give will never contradict the message of the Bible.

Going through life not knowing him is like sailing across the Pacific Ocean with no maps or equipment. So, if you are ready to begin your own journey to the core and you don't know the Lord, I'd like to introduce you:

"Lord, this reader is ready for you to forgive them, guide them and venture through the remainder of their lives with you. Thank you for your unconditional love, your sacrificial death and your willingness to do this for all no matter where we have wondered or what we have done. Thank you for hearing their prayer."

There is no magic formula or perfectly worded prayer that makes the connection rather it is your heartfelt belief Jesus did all this for you and you are ready for him to come into your life and do the journey with you. Jesus always responds to the seeking person and will promise to lead you on this journey as you learn to follow him. If you are ready, you may let him know by saying something like this to him in prayer.

"Lord, where do I begin? I need you; I want you in my life. Thank you for dying so I could be forgiven, and I want forgiveness! I am a little afraid but believe you want my best, so I will trust you. I accept you, and I want to know and follow you, in Jesus name, Amen."

If you have made this decision, your journey to the core has begun! The Lord can already see you as totally complete, healthy and living from a redeemed core. He simply invites you to follow him as he shapes you toward what he already sees you will become.

APPENDIX B
REVIEW EACH CHAPTER IN A COUPLE OF SENTENCES

1. The concept of the core is explained. The core is that deep place of wounding in us that hides the true core given to us by God.
2. The circle of responsibility is the powerful concept focusing us on what is our responsibility and to grasp it with gusto.
3. Explores the three realms of buried pain. Our spiritual disconnection, our emotional wounds, and our physical imperfections all effects of the original fall, all cause us great pain.
4. The three layers of protection are revealed and how we attempt to appear to others and often ourselves better than we know we are.
5. Rather than some specific failure, this chapter begins to see key lies we all believe and society supports. This chapter examines the message I am not loveable.
6. Continuing the lies, this chapter explores the feeling I am not acceptable. If you knew me, you wouldn't accept me.
7. Especially crippling for men is the lie I am not adequate. I don't measure up; I don't have what it takes.
8. The hurt family tree explores why it is critical on this journey to learn how to deal with hurt before it grows to resentments and finally bitterness.

9. This chapter was a major discovery for me, the buried treasure that at the core I am not dark with shame but rather white with God's decree.

10. Buried treasure number one countering the enemies lies! I am loved.

11. Treasure number two I am acceptable.

12. Finally, treasure number three I have everything I need to do whatever God desires.

13. What an amazing chapter seeing the areas where we had the most shame and guilt when redeemed become the very platform for God to use us in the lives of others.

14. A stunning reality is when we get healed up and begin doing a genuine heart to heart ministry the enemy fears us.

15. Living the authentic life so what you see is me comes when the journey to the core has been taken, and all the hidden parts have been brought to life, redeemed and now used by God.

16. Your last vote is about surrendering your right to order your own life, choosing rather let the Lord direct your journey.

17. Living from the core means learning to love, learning to love God and love people.

18. To love, I need also learn to listen so I know how to answer the question what would love require of me in this situation. Listening for the promptings answering that question is how we learn to love.

19. The promptings ask me to give something of myself whether my time, involvement or something that cost money.

20. This authentic lifestyle causes me to notice the blessings of God more fully in my life and provoke praise to him and for his gifts.

21. This chapter clarifies the concept of having a testimony. Your testimony isn't really about you; it is about the gifts God has given and how he is shaping your life. Tell what he is doing in you rather than what someone else needs him to do in them.

ENDNOTES

[1] Dr. Keith Ablow, MD, *Living the Truth:* (New York, NY: Little Brown and Company Hachette Book Group USA, 2007), 38

[2] Reinhold Neibuhr included this prayer in a sermon in 1943: God, give me grace to accept with serenity

the things that cannot be changed, Courage to change the things which should be changed, and the Wisdom to distinguish the one from the other. Living one day at a time, Enjoying one moment at a time, Accepting hardship as a pathway to peace, Taking, as Jesus did, This sinful world as it is,

Not as I would have it, Trusting that You will make all things right, If I surrender to Your will,

So that I may be reasonably happy in this life, And supremely happy with You forever in the next.

Amen.

[3] You can learn more about Liz Murray at www.homelesstoharvard.com.

[4] http://www.talkingaboutmenshealth.com/2010/06/17/passivity-and-the-male-psyche/

[5] https://www.usatoday.com/story/news/nation-now/2017/04/12/americans-spending-more-than-ever-plastic-surgery/100365258/

[6] Matthew 23, Jesus scathing rebuke of the practice of developing religious layers of protection.

[7] In arguing his point about being able to be proud about religious accomplishments, Paul lists his heritage. He was circumcised on the eight days, his family line was pure, he was from Benjamin's tribe, he was an elite Jew.

[8] Philippians 3:10

9 John 4:

10 Genesis 3

11 Why I Stayed: The Choices I Made In My Darkest Hour, Gayle Haggard, Tyndale 2010

12 Galatians 5:22-23

13 Ephesians 4:32

14 Genesis 1:26 "So God created people in his own image; God patterned them after himself; male and female he created them."

15 John 14:9 Jesus said, "Anyone who has seen e has seen the Father! Also, Hebrews 1:3 states Jesus was the exact image of God.

16 Read carefully Romans 3:19-26 preferably in the New Living Translation

17 John 3:17

18 1 Peter 3:15

19 Romans 12:6-8; 1 Corinthians 12-14

20 Alcoholics Anonymous and Narcotics Anonymous twelve step programs

21 *The Twelve Steps A Spiritual Journey, A Working Guide For Healing Damaged Emotions,* (RGI Publishing, Inc. Julian, CA) 1988, 1994.

22 I like the term! It means basically to have two things in your mind that you cannot harmonize. For me it was my actions clearly were a violation of my belief system. The weight of attempting to justify was brutal.

23 Merriam-Webster Online Dictionary

24 Celebrate Recovery was started at Saddleback Church by a man named John Baker. You can learn more at www.saddlebackresources.com

25 John 3:2ff.

26 Cloud, Henry. Integrity: The Courage to Meet the Demands of Reality. New York: 2006. p. 73

27 Tyndale House Publishers. (2007). *Holy Bible: New Living Translation.* (3rd ed.) (Jn 4:17–18). Carol Stream, IL: Tyndale House Publishers.

28 Tyndale House Publishers. (2007). *Holy Bible: New Living Translation.* (3rd ed.) (Jn 4:28–30). Carol Stream, IL: Tyndale House Publishers.

29 See 1 John 3:1-2

30 See Philippians 1:6

31 See 2 Timothy 4:1-2

32 Eldredge, John. "Wild at Heart: Discovering the Secret of a Man's Soul." Nashville, Tennessee: 2001 & 2010. P. 168.

---

[33] www.merriam-webster.com

[34] The Johari Window was developed by Joseph Luft and Harry Ingham in the 1950's. They combined their first to names Joe and Harry to come up with Johari. The tool is used widely today to teach soft skills concerning awareness, disclosure and feedback.

[35] 1 John :9 and James 5:16 In essence the 4th and 5th steps of a twelve step program.

[36] Romans 12:1-2 & Ephesians 2:8-10

[37] Andy Stanley is the founding pastor of North Point Community Church in Atlanta, GA. Andy is the son of Dr. Charles Stanley. North Point Ministries has given birth to several other church campuses and is one of the most influential ministries in the world.

[38] Philippians 2:3

[39] www.Northpoint.org/messages

[40] John 13:34-35

[41] Parnitha Timothy is the director of aftercare, International Justice Mission and she serves in Chennai, India. She has survived a brain tumor that has impacted her voice. She speaks very softly but has such an attractive joy.

[42] Written by John Lynch, Bruce McNicol and Bill Thrall. www.truefaced.com

[43] Matthew 16:26
[44] Matthew 6:19
[45] Mark 7:8-13
[46] Matthew 6:21
[47] John 15:5
[48] John 10:10
[49] Matthew 12:34b
[50] Matthew 23

Contact The Author:

If you have questions or comments or would like the author to speak to your group, he can be reached at scottranck1@gmail.com

Made in the USA
Middletown, DE
27 September 2023

39564686R00087